MONETARY, FISCAL AND TRADE POLICIES

INTERNATIONAL LABOR GRANTS

U.S. MANAGEMENT AND MONITORING EFFORTS

MONETARY, FISCAL AND TRADE POLICIES

Additional books in this series can be found on Nova's website under the Series tab.

Additional e-books in this series can be found on Nova's website under the e-book tab.

MONETARY, FISCAL AND TRADE POLICIES

INTERNATIONAL LABOR GRANTS

U.S. MANAGEMENT AND MONITORING EFFORTS

CRISTINA M. PORTER
EDITOR

New York

Library of Congress Cataloging-in-Publication Data

ISBN: 978-1-63482-398-2

Published by Nova Science Publishers, Inc. † New York

CONTENTS

PREFACE

This book examines how ILAB develops its technical assistance projects; how ILAB selects recipients of its funding; and how the Department of Labor manages its grant award documentation.

Chapter 1 – Recent incidents, including the collapse of a factory building in Bangladesh, have highlighted poor working conditions overseas. According to the International Labour Organization, millions of children worldwide are engaged in labor that hinders their development. ILAB provides technical assistance mainly through international and nongovernmental organizations to improve working conditions by supporting worker rights and combating child labor. You asked us to review issues related to ILAB's international technical assistance. This report examines (1) how ILAB develops its technical assistance projects, (2) how ILAB selects recipients of its funding, and (3) how Labor manages its grant award documentation.

To address these objectives, GAO reviewed Labor guidance on procurement, ILAB project manager manuals, and grant solicitations. GAO examined a nongeneralizable sample of 26 award files that were active in calendar years 2011-2013. GAO selected this sample based on several factors, including dollar value and geographic location. GAO also interviewed officials from ILAB and the Labor procurement office as well as ILAB grantees in Washington, D.C.

Chapter 2 – According to the International Labour Organization, millions of children worldwide are engaged in labor that hinders their development. Recent incidents, including a factory collapse in Bangladesh, have highlighted poor working conditions overseas. ILAB's child labor office and trade and labor office provide funding to improve working conditions by supporting worker rights and combating child labor, mainly through international and nongovernmental organizations. The child labor office obligated about $56 million and the trade and labor office obligated about $13.5 million in fiscal year 2013. You asked us to review issues related to ILAB's international technical assistance. This report examines how ILAB (1) ensures the financial accountability of its technical assistance funds, (2) monitors the performance of its projects, and (3) evaluates its projects and uses the results of the evaluations. To address these objectives, GAO reviewed ILAB documents on financial requirements, performance monitoring, and evaluation. GAO analyzed a nongeneralizable sample of 26 grants that were active in calendar years 2011-2013. GAO selected this sample based on several factors, including dollar value and geographic location.

In: International Labor Grants
Editor: Cristina M. Porter

ISBN: 978-1-63482-398-2

Chapter 1

INTERNATIONAL LABOR GRANTS: LABOR SHOULD IMPROVE MANAGEMENT OF KEY AWARD DOCUMENTATION*

United States Government Accountability Office

ABBREVIATIONS

ILO	International Labour Organization
ILAB	Bureau of International Labor Affairs
Labor	Department of Labor
OCFT	Office of Child Labor, Forced Labor, and Human Trafficking
OMB	Office of Management and Budget
OTLA	Office of Trade and Labor Affairs
State	Department of State
USAID	U.S. Agency for International Development

WHY GAO DID THIS STUDY

Recent incidents, including the collapse of a factory building in Bangladesh, have highlighted poor working conditions overseas. According to

* This is an edited, reformatted and augmented version of The United States Government Accountability Office publication, GAO-14-493, dated May 2014.

the International Labour Organization, millions of children worldwide are engaged in labor that hinders their development. ILAB provides technical assistance mainly through international and nongovernmental organizations to improve working conditions by supporting worker rights and combating child labor. You asked us to review issues related to ILAB's international technical assistance. This report examines (1) how ILAB develops its technical assistance projects, (2) how ILAB selects recipients of its funding, and (3) how Labor manages its grant award documentation.

To address these objectives, GAO reviewed Labor guidance on procurement, ILAB project manager manuals, and grant solicitations. GAO examined a nongeneralizable sample of 26 award files that were active in calendar years 2011-2013. GAO selected this sample based on several factors, including dollar value and geographic location. GAO also interviewed officials from ILAB and the Labor procurement office as well as ILAB grantees in Washington, D.C.

What GAO Recommends

To ensure the integrity of the procurement process for ILAB grants, the Secretary of Labor should provide guidance about documents required in grant award files and ensure that the guidance is implemented. Labor agreed with the recommendations.

What GAO Found

The Department of Labor's (Labor) Bureau of International Labor Affairs (ILAB) has guidance and criteria for developing projects covering trade and labor and child labor. In fiscal year 2013, the child labor office obligated about \$56 million and the trade and labor office obligated about \$13.5 million for technical assistance projects. Officials from both offices said they consider many factors in deciding where to provide technical assistance, including the nature and extent of the problem, U.S. government priorities, and host government commitment. Each office uses a variety of information sources to develop project ideas. Once ILAB has decided to develop a project, the draft grant solicitation must go through Labor's agency-wide clearance process.

Labor has established procedures to select recipients of its funding, including processes for evaluating applications for grants, such as assessing applicants' past performance and capacity to manage grant funds. Officials said they have difficulty attracting a large number of applicants because the pool is potentially constrained by the specialized nature of the work, challenging location of the grants, and size and complexity of the grants. According to officials, ILAB takes steps to maximize competition, such as publishing Notices of Intent to give applicants more time to develop proposals.

Incomplete documentation makes it difficult to determine if Labor is following its grant award procedures, including conducting due diligence on financial viability and past performance of applicants. Based on GAO's review of 26 grant award files, over half of the files were missing some documentation, and 4 were missing all pre-award documents (see figure). Officials said that the procurement office has been trying to improve the organization of the files so that it is easier to follow the steps of the award process. For example, procurement officials said they are trying to more consistently use a checklist to record the documents the office receives, such as past performance information. However, use of this checklist is not required, and Labor guidance does not clearly state what documents must be retained in award files. According to *Standards for Internal Control in the Federal Government*, internal control, all transactions, and other significant events need to be clearly documented, and the documentation should be readily available. Further, the standards state that all documentation and records should be properly managed and maintained. Without such assurance that Labor is following its grant award procedures, ILAB is at increased risk of not meeting the goals of its programs.

Summary of key documents found in 26 award files

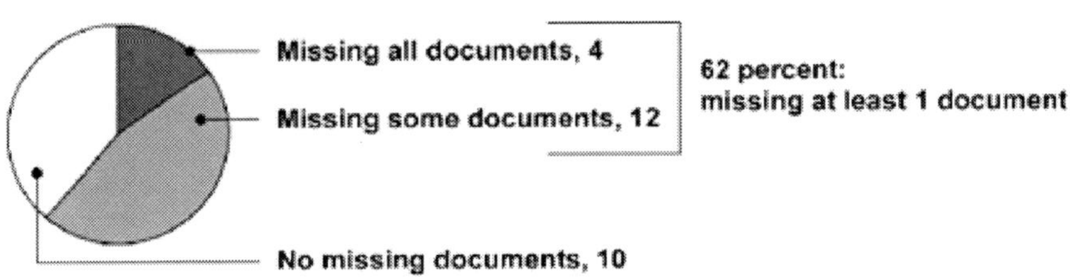

Source: GAO analysis of Department of Labor data.

* * *

May 15, 2014

The Honorable Orrin G. Hatch
Ranking Member
Senate Committee on Finance

The Honorable Lamar Alexander
Ranking Member
Senate Committee on Health, Education, Labor and Pensions

Recent incidents, including the collapse of a garment factory building in Bangladesh,[1] have highlighted poor working conditions overseas. In addition, according to the International Labour Organization (ILO),[2] millions of children worldwide are engaged in labor that hinders their education, development, and future livelihoods. In response to concerns about working conditions for children and adults, the U.S. government, in part through the Department of Labor's (Labor) Bureau of International Labor Affairs (ILAB), provides technical assistance mainly through international and nongovernmental organizations to improve working conditions by supporting worker rights and combating child labor.

You asked us to review issues related to ILAB's international technical assistance. This report examines (1) how ILAB develops its technical assistance projects, (2) how ILAB selects recipients of its funding, and (3) how Labor manages its grant award documentation. We will be issuing an additional report at a later date that addresses financial and performance monitoring and evaluation.

To address these objectives, we reviewed relevant documents, including Labor guidance on procurement, ILAB project manager manuals, and grant solicitations. In addition, we developed a data collection instrument that we used to review a sample of award files for ILAB projects. We selected a nongeneralizable sample of 26 projects out of a total of 98 projects that were active in calendar years 2011, 2012, and 2013.[3] We selected the sample based on several factors, such as dollar value and geographic location. The sample represents about 44 percent of ILAB funding over these years and includes 7 of the 9 grants with the highest dollar value ($10 million or above). Our sample includes projects that are single-country; multicountry; completed; ongoing; direct services; capacity building; and in most geographic regions.

We also discussed ILAB's processes for developing project ideas and awarding grants with officials from ILAB and the procurement office in Labor's Office of the Assistant Secretary for Administration and Management. In addition, we discussed these processes with ILAB grantees in Washington, D.C., and during field work in Cambodia, Ecuador, Peru, and Thailand. We selected these locations based on, among other factors, size of grant, geographic location, and phase of the project. Appendix I provides more information about our scope and methodology.

We conducted this performance audit from June 2013 to May 2014 in accordance with generally accepted government auditing standards. Those standards require that we plan and perform the audit to obtain sufficient, appropriate evidence to provide a reasonable basis for our findings and conclusions based on our audit objectives. We believe that the evidence obtained provides a reasonable basis for our findings and conclusions based on our audit objectives.

BACKGROUND

The mission of ILAB involves improving working conditions, promoting workers' rights, and addressing the workplace exploitation of children and other vulnerable populations overseas. This work is carried out by its Office of Child Labor, Forced Labor, and Human Trafficking (OCFT, referred to here as the child labor office) and its Office of Trade and Labor Affairs (OTLA, referred to here as the trade and labor office), through projects developed and funded by the offices and generally implemented by international or nongovernmental organizations. Figure 1 shows the structure of the ILAB office. In fiscal year 2013, Congress appropriated about $66.5 million to ILAB for international technical assistance provided that "$40 million shall be for programs to combat exploitative child labor internationally" and "not less than $6.5 million shall be used to implement model programs that address worker rights issues."[4] Of that amount, the child labor office obligated about $56 million, and the trade and labor office obligated about $6.5 million for technical assistance projects.[5] From fiscal year 2011 through fiscal year 2013, ILAB obligated about $225 million. During that time the child labor office obligated about $176 million and the trade and labor office obligated about $49 million.[6]

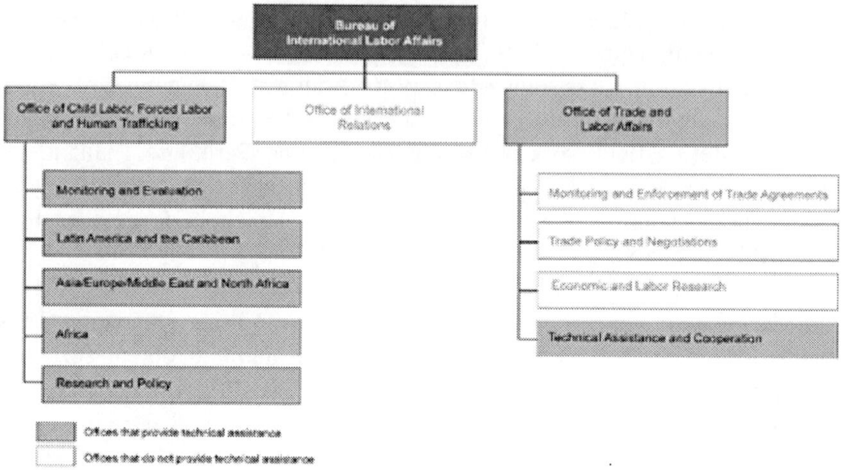

Source: Department of Labor.

Figure 1. Bureau of International Labor Affairs Organization Chart with Offices That Provide Technical Assistance.

The child labor office's technical assistance includes direct educational services, capacity building, and supporting research on international child labor, forced labor, and human trafficking. Among other responsibilities, the office funds and oversees cooperative agreements and contracts to organizations engaged in efforts to eliminate exploitative child labor around the world. It funded 40 projects between fiscal years 2011 and 2013. For example, in fiscal year 2011, the office funded a $13 million project to combat rural exploitative child labor in Peru that included education services, livelihoods assistance, and research on child labor.

The trade and labor office's technical assistance focuses on projects to improve worker rights. It funded 34 projects between fiscal years 2011 and 2013. For example, in fiscal year 2011 the office provided $1 million to improve labor compliance in the footwear industry in Cambodia and to improve the capacity of labor law enforcement.

Labor Has Guidance for Developing ILAB Grant Solicitations

ILAB has guidance and criteria for developing project ideas. Officials from both the trade and labor office and child labor office told us the criteria are not formally weighted and that they consider many factors in deciding where to provide technical assistance, including the nature and extent of the problem, U.S. government priorities, and host government commitment. Before ILAB can publish a grant solicitation, it must go through Labor's agency-wide clearance process.

ILAB Has Guidance and Several Criteria for Developing Project Ideas

The child labor and trade and labor offices each have general guidance for developing project ideas, including guidance on stakeholder involvement and identifying targets of opportunity. In addition, the trade and labor office guidance includes templates for assessing initial project ideas. Both offices have several high-level criteria for project development, including sustainability and host government commitment. (See appendix II for the full list of criteria.)

Each office uses a variety of information sources to develop potential projects. Officials from the trade and labor office said they identify potential project ideas using information from other office divisions, including submissions filed under free trade agreements.[7] In addition, they said they consult with relevant stakeholders, such as the Office of the U.S. Trade Representative, the U.S. Agency for International Development (USAID), the Department of State (State), and U.S. embassies. Officials from the child labor office told us they develop potential project ideas based on information collected from the office's research on the three annual reports on international child labor and forced labor they produce,[8] as well as discussions with various stakeholders inside and outside Labor, such as USAID, State, U.S. embassies, and others.

According to ILAB officials, they can consider additional factors when developing projects, including leadership priorities. They told us that ILAB's formal leadership priorities are outlined in its annual operation plan and 5-year strategic plan. ILAB officials said that office directors from both the trade and labor office and child labor office meet every week with the office of the deputy undersecretary for international affairs to discuss issues. For example, trade and labor office officials told us a current priority is building the capacity of other governments to enforce their labor laws by, for instance, improving the capacity and skills of labor inspectors. Officials also said that if there is a significant event, such as the garment factory fires and factory collapse in Bangladesh, their priorities can adjust to reflect new situations. In addition, officials from the child labor office said that in the 1990s, they funded projects targeting child soldiers and commercial sexual exploitation. However, they found that to have greater impact, they needed to develop projects that intervene earlier, before children become soldiers or sex workers. Officials told us they have increased their focus on prevention in addition to removing children from child labor.

ILAB officials said the criteria they use for project development and selection are not formally weighted and the importance of individual criteria can vary depending on the situation. For example, ILAB officials told us that regardless of the severity of a problem, they generally do not provide assistance in a country where the government does not welcome an ILAB project.[9] ILAB officials told us they look for opportunities for discernible impact and likelihood of success. They define success as not only meeting the goals of the project, but also developing strategies that could be applied more widely.[10] Officials from the child labor office told us that their main criterion is the nature and extent of exploitative child labor,[11] but other factors can take precedence in determining where to provide technical assistance. For example, they do not necessarily target their assistance to the countries with the highest incidences of child labor or with the worst forms of child labor. The projects we reviewed, for instance, include countries where the percentage of children working varies from about 7 percent in Panama to 50 percent in Ethiopia, according to recent statistics in ILAB's Findings on the Worst Forms of Child Labor.[12] However, child labor officials said that, even taking into account other factors, their projects generally result in a focus on the worst forms of child labor or hazardous work. For example, of the six solicitations for direct services in our sample that were posted in 2011 and 2012, half explicitly mention children engaged in the "worst form of child labor" or "hazardous work" as the target population. Although the other half of solicitations did not explicitly use these terms, the solicitations described working conditions that fall under the definition of hazardous work.[13]

Labor Has an Agency-wide Clearance Process for Grant Solicitations

ILAB has a review process for developing and approving potential projects and grant solicitations. According to ILAB officials, project managers on both trade and labor and child labor grants develop a list of potential projects using the criteria and information discussed above. The office division chiefs review and refine the list and provide project recommendations to the directors of each of the offices. The office directors further refine the list of recommended projects, which they give to the deputy undersecretary for international affairs for final selection. In 2013, officials estimated that child labor project managers developed around 20 project proposals (including country-specific projects, research projects, and monitoring and evaluation projects), 15 of which were submitted to the deputy undersecretary, and 12 of those are under consideration. Officials estimated that trade and labor project managers developed around 20 project ideas, 8 of which were forwarded to the deputy undersecretary, and 6 of those are under consideration.

Competitive Award Process Steps

- Notice of Intent
- Solicitation for grant applications
- Application pre-screening
- Evaluation panel application review
- Grant award decision
- Notification of award decision

Source: ILAB.

According to ILAB guidance, once a potential project is approved, project managers conduct a needs assessment to further develop the project idea and write the scope of work for the grant solicitation. The needs assessment can be comprised of different efforts depending on the situation; for example, it could involve desk research and a visit to the target country to help determine the scope of each project. ILAB guidance also states that they will consult with stakeholders, including other U.S. government agencies and the U.S. embassy in the target country, and obtain written approval from the host country government to implement the project. According to ILAB guidance, Labor publishes a Notice of Intent on the grants.gov web portal to notify the public and potential bidders that ILAB intends to issue a solicitation. According to ILAB officials, project managers then write the scope of work for the solicitation, which they send to the child labor and trade and labor office directors for approval. According to officials, the scope of work identifies the problem to be addressed, while the applicant should propose the way to address the problem. After the ILAB office directors approve the solicitation, according to officials, it is sent to the deputy undersecretary for international affairs for clearance, then to all agencies in Labor for review and comment, and clearance by the office of the executive secretary. Finally, the solicitation for grant applications is published on grants.gov.

LABOR HAS ESTABLISHED PROCEDURES TO SELECT ILAB GRANTEES BUT HAS FACED CHALLENGES IN MAXIMIZING COMPETITION

Labor has established procedures to evaluate competitive and noncompetitive applications for cooperative agreements. In addition, noncompetitive grants need approval from the Labor Procurement Review Board. ILAB has faced challenges in maximizing competition, broadening the pool of organizations that apply for grants, because that pool is potentially constrained by the specialized nature of the work, challenging location of grants, and size and complexity of the grants. ILAB officials told us they take steps to maximize competition, including writing scopes of work that are broad enough for an applicant to develop its own strategy and publishing Notices of Intent to give applicants more time to develop proposals.

For competitive solicitations, once the application deadline has passed, a grant officer in Labor's procurement office conducts a review of the applications to determine whether applicants have met all requirements to be eligible for award consideration. According to Labor officials, in 2011, the procurement office began using a responsiveness review checklist to determine whether documents required in the solicitation are included in the application file. For example, the checklist contains fields for whether the applicant submitted technical and cost proposals; past performance information; an audit opinion letter and summary of findings; and whether the applicant is registered in the System for Award Management,[14] which includes information on excluded parties.[15] Applications found eligible by the procurement office are provided to a technical evaluation panel for review and evaluation.

Labor Has Procedures for Awarding Competitive and NonCompetitive Grants

ILAB selects and identifies the technical evaluation panel members and chair. According to ILAB officials, the panel chair is often the project manager who developed the solicitation. The panel chair is responsible for, among other things, ensuring compliance with proceedings, applicable regulations, and solicitation requirements; keeping a record of panel proceedings; and submitting a record of the proceedings of the panel to the procurement office. The individual panelists are each responsible for reading and completing evaluations for all applications. ILAB officials said that influence of the panel chair is moderated by the other panel members, and that the chair's role is to facilitate and organize the process, not to dictate the review. ILAB panels generally include three to four people, including the chair. ILAB officials said that the other panelists can be people from within the agency who have expertise on the sector or country, as well as people from outside of Labor, such as academics or the State desk officer for the country. Labor officials said the procurement office provides training to panelists. The most recent training document, from July 2013, includes an integrity overview, including confidentiality and conflict of interest provisions, and explains the process the panel follows during the evaluation of the applications.

Competitive Award Process Steps

- Notice of Intent issued
- Solicitation for grant applications
- Application pre-screening
- Evaluation panel application review
- Grant award decision
- Notification of award decision

Source: ILAB.

Each panelist evaluates all applications using a rating form developed for each solicitation based on criteria and point values outlined in the solicitation.[16] Each panelist's individual evaluations are summarized in the panel consensus report, which provides an award recommendation to the procurement office. The panel uses a competitive range, established prior to the review of the applications, in its evaluation process to screen out applicants that do not achieve a minimum point value. According to ILAB officials, the main criteria they use to evaluate applications are (1) project design and budget, (2) organizational capacity, and (3) personnel and project management. The point value assigned to each criterion varies across solicitations depending on the type of project; for example, a global project may assign more points to organizational capacity than a single country project. Applicants' past performance is assessed under the organizational capacity criterion. The procurement office asks the panel chair for questions to send to the applicants' references and then provides the references' answers on past performance to the evaluation panel. Officials also said that they assess the management systems and capacity of applicants to manage grant funds during the panel evaluation by examining the audit submitted by the applicant, budget narrative and outputs-based budget, past performance, management structure for the project, and organizational capacity. The procurement office makes the final award decision and notifies the grantee. Of the eight competitive solicitations we reviewed that received more than one applicant, the highest rated applicant always received the grant award. The two competitive solicitations in our sample with only one applicant met the minimum point value for awarding the grant.

Non-Competitive Award Process Steps

- Procurement Review Board review and approval
- Notice of Intent to sole source
- Scope of award to grantee
- Budget and plans from grantee
- Notification of award decision

Source: ILAB.

For noncompetitive awards—grant awards made using less than full and open competition—ILAB needs approval from the procurement office and the Labor Procurement Review Board. Of the 26 award files we reviewed, ILAB awarded 12 grants noncompetitively. Nine of the noncompetitive grants were child labor grants, and three focused on trade and labor.[17] According to ILAB officials, if ILAB determines that there is only one organization that can implement a project, the first step is an internal ILAB review followed by reviews conducted by the deputy undersecretary for international affairs and the procurement office. The request for a noncompetitive or limited competition award is then sent to the Labor Procurement Review Board which is composed of representatives from various Labor offices. The board evaluates the request against the Department of Labor Management Series criteria for exclusions and exceptions to competitive procedures for grants and cooperative agreements, and it has to meet at least one of the criteria—for example, that a noncompetitive award is authorized or required by the statute funding the program. The board makes a recommendation to the chief acquisition officer, who has the final determination. Labor posts a Notice of Intent to sole source on grants.gov. ILAB then provides the scope of award to the grantee, obtains the budget and work plans from the grantees, and finally notifies the grantee of the award decision. Officials said that when ILAB received congressionally directed funding for the ILO, it still was required to follow this process.[18]

ILAB Has Faced Challenges in Maximizing Competition for Its Grants, but Has Taken Steps to Increase Competition

ILAB officials stated that they face challenges in maximizing competition but have taken steps to address them. Of the 26 award files we reviewed, ILAB awarded 14 grants competitively. Of these 14 competitive solicitations, we found evidence that 7 solicitations received 3 or more applications, and 1 solicitation received 2 applications, while 2 solicitations received only 1 application each.[19]

According to ILAB officials, they face challenges in maximizing competition, as their pool of applicants is potentially constrained by the nature of the work, location of grants, and size of grants. Officials from the trade and labor office said that the work ILAB does is specialized, and there are not many organizations that have the experience or the capacity to, for example, train labor inspectors. In addition, child labor grants, have many different components, such as direct services, research, and capacity building. In addition, the difficult implementing environment for some projects decreases the pool of applicants. For example, it can be difficult to find organizations that are willing to work in environments that are remote, contain security concerns, or lack basic infrastructure. Furthermore, according to ILAB officials, the size and complexity of grants are based on several factors, including ensuring that the grant has sufficient resources to address the problems identified in the solicitation. Moreover, according to ILAB officials, large grants are generally the same amount of work and involve the same procedures to develop and oversee as small grants. ILAB officials said that some potential grantees stated that ILAB's grants were too large for their organization. Those grantees said they had the capacity to manage a $100,000 grant but not a $10 million grant, which generally has a large multifaceted scope that will be implemented in multiple locations. The size and complexity of these types of grants can be difficult for some organizations to manage.[20]

ILAB officials told us they take a variety of steps to try to maximize competition, including increasing the period of time that the solicitation is open; holding webinars to answer questions while the solicitation is open; and writing scopes of work that are broad enough for applicants to design their own strategy.

Officials said that giving applicants more time to develop proposals can increase competition. For example, the Notice of Intent gives potential applicants an advance announcement that a solicitation is likely to follow. In addition, ILAB officials said that they try to keep the solicitation open as long as possible, a minimum of 30 days, to allow more time for applicants to develop proposals. Several grantee officials we spoke with noted the importance of having enough time to develop their applications because it allows them to produce better proposals. One grantee official told us that the Notices of Intent that ILAB has been posting before the official solicitation have been very helpful. Another grantee official told us that the rules for submitting proposals are very clear, but the process is expensive and rigorous, so having experience with the issues, contacts, and a relationship with the host country government is useful in quickly figuring out where to focus the proposal.

After the solicitation is issued, ILAB holds a webinar to answer questions. A grantee official we spoke with noted that ILAB has improved the question and answer process.

Finally, ILAB officials told us they try to write the solicitation scope of work broadly enough to describe the problem the project is trying to address but leave room for applicants to design their own strategy. Labor's solicitor's office provides comments on whether the solicitation is too narrow.

INCOMPLETE AWARD FILE DOCUMENTATION CAUSES UNCERTAINTY ABOUT WHETHER LABOR FOLLOWED ITS PROCEDURES

Incomplete documentation makes it difficult to determine if Labor has established internal controls over, and is following, its grant award procedures,[21] including ensuring that Labor does not award grants to organizations that have been debarred from doing business with the federal government. Our review of 26 grant award files showed that some key pre-award documentation was missing in over half of the files and 4 files were missing all pre-award documents. According to officials, all awards are required to go through these steps, regardless of the number of applications received or whether the grant was awarded noncompetitively. Similarly, a March 2012 Labor Inspector General report found Labor contract files were missing key documents.[22] Lack of readily available documentation causes uncertainty about whether Labor followed all of its procedures. Without such assurance, achieved through sufficient internal controls, that Labor is following its grant award procedures, ILAB is at increased risk of not meeting the goals of its programs. Figure 2 shows the prevalence of key documents in 26 award files.

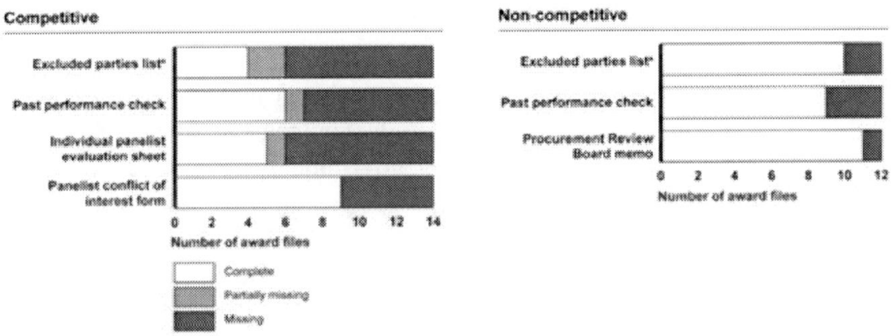

Source: GAO analysis of Department of Labor data.

[a] An excluded party, subject to certain exceptions, is a person who is excluded by any federal agency and may not: (a) be a participant in certain federal agency transactions or (b) act as a principal of a person participating in one of those transactions. Transactions include grants, cooperative agreements, loans, and subsidies. 2 C.F.R. §§ 180.130 and 180.970.

Note: "Partially missing" refers to files in which documents were missing for some, but not all, applicants.

Figure 2. Complete, Partially Missing, and Missing Key Documents in 26 Award Files.

Key documents that would provide evidence that required procedures were being followed, but which were missing in some or all of the grant award files we reviewed, include:

- *Individual evaluation sheets:* for competitive awards, document the rating and assessment of applicants by each panelist.

  - Of the 14 competitive award files we reviewed, 8 files were missing all individual evaluation sheets; 1 file was missing 1 individual evaluation sheet; and 5 files contained all individual evaluation sheets.
- *Conflict of interest forms*: for competitive awards, provide support that the individual panelist does not have a conflict or appearance of conflict with the applicants.
  - Of the 14 competitive award files we reviewed, 9 contained documentation stating that the panelists evaluating the applications did not have a conflict of interest, and 5 files were missing this documentation.
- *Labor Procurement Review Board approval:* required for noncompetitive awards.
  - Of the 12 noncompetitive award files we reviewed, 11 contained documentation of the Labor Procurement Review Board approval in the individual or umbrella project files. For 1 file, the Procurement Review Board approval was for a no-cost extension of the project but not for the original agreement.
- *Excluded parties list:* for competitive and noncompetitive awards, indicates whether an applicant is suspended or debarred.
  - Of the 14 competitive award files we reviewed, 4 files had evidence that Labor searched the excluded parties list; 8 files were missing that evidence; and 2 files had results for the excluded parties list search for some but not all applicants.
  - Of the 12 noncompetitive awards, 10 files had evidence in the individual or umbrella project file that Labor searched the excluded parties list and 2 files were missing that evidence.
- *Past performance:* for competitive and noncompetitive awards, can provide information on whether the applicant has a history of poor performance.
  - Of the 14 competitive solicitation files we reviewed, 6 files had evidence Labor had checked past performance; 7 were missing evidence of past performance checks; and 1 had evidence for only one of the applicants.
  - Of the 12 noncompetitive solicitation files we reviewed, 3 were missing evidence of a past performance check. Two files specifically referred to the past good performance of the implementer in the memo to the Procurement Review Board. Seven files listed past projects implemented by the organization in

> the memo to the Procurement Review Board. We accepted these as evidence of checking past performance.

According to Labor officials, the procurement office keeps all documents for the winning grantee, including the consensus report from the grant evaluation panel. However, after the debriefing period has ended,[23] it does not keep the individual panelist's review sheets from the grant evaluation panel or the unsuccessful applications. According to Labor officials, they follow Labor's record retention regulation,[24] which pertains to documents related to grantees and sub-grantees. Specifically, the regulation applies to "all financial and programmatic records, supporting documents, statistical records, and other records of grantees or subgrantees which are (i) required to be maintained by the terms of this part, program regulations or the grant agreement, or (ii) otherwise reasonably considered as pertinent to program regulations or the grant agreement."[25] However, the regulation does not specifically name documents such as the excluded parties list or past performance documentation. While Labor does have more specific guidance for retaining documents for contract awards, it does not have guidance on retaining specific documents for the grant award process. For example, a 2013 procurement memo requires, as a best practice, that contract specialists and officers maintain excluded parties verification results in award files. Because the procurement office handles both contracts and grants, officials said they try to apply similar principles to both contracts and grants. According to officials, they keep documents related to the award itself, such as the solicitation, the successful submitted application, and its related evaluation consensus report.

Labor officials acknowledged that many grant award files were missing documents, and the office has been trying to improve the organization of the files so that it is easier to follow the sequence of the award process. For example, the procurement office is now trying to more consistently use the responsiveness review checklist to record the documents it receives from applicants as well as another checklist to record the documents in the award files. However, neither of these checklists is an official requirement. According to Standards for Internal Control in the Federal Government, internal control and all transactions and other significant events need to be clearly documented, and the documentation should be readily available for examination. Further, the standards state that all documentation and records should be properly managed and maintained.[26] Internal control helps the government effectively manage and safeguard resources.

CONCLUSION

Congress funds the child labor and trade and labor offices to, among other things, address the conditions that could lead to disasters such as the factory collapse in Bangladesh and the tragedy of millions of children around the world facing harsh employment conditions and missing out on educational opportunities. To implement one of Labor's aims of improving working conditions overseas by supporting worker rights and combating child labor, it is important that they select grantees that have the financial and technical capacity to carry out these projects, ensuring that applicants are qualified to participate in the grant award process. While Labor has processes for developing projects and selecting grantees, incomplete documentation in award files makes it unclear if Labor followed those processes. Labor has issued guidance for retaining specific documents for awarding contracts but does not have guidance on retaining specific documents for grant awards. Labor is therefore not able to demonstrate that the grant award process has been conducted according to procedures. Internal control, which is synonymous with management control, helps government program managers achieve desired results through effective stewardship of public resources. Internal control serves as the first line of defense in safeguarding assets and preventing and detecting errors and fraud, including ensuring that Labor does not award grants to organizations that have been debarred from doing business with the federal government. Without such assurance that Labor is following its grant award procedures, these programs are at increased risk of not meeting the goals of improving working conditions, protecting workers' ability to exercise their rights, and addressing the workplace exploitation of children and other vulnerable populations.

RECOMMENDATIONS FOR EXECUTIVE ACTION

To ensure the integrity of the procurement process for ILAB grants, the Secretary of Labor should:

1) provide guidance as to what documents should be in the grant award files to show that all grant award requirements were met; and
2) establish a mechanism to ensure that the guidance is implemented.

Agency Comments and Our Evaluation

We provided a draft of this report to Labor for comment. We also provided relevant text to State for technical comments.

In its written comments, Labor agreed with the recommendations and stated that it will continue to work to improve its grant making process. Labor also described steps that it has taken to address concerns similar to those reflected in the report, including the creation of a responsiveness review checklist and application package checklist. We recognize that these are steps that may improve the documentation of Labor's grant award process. However, as noted in our report, neither of these checklists is an official requirement codified in the agency's polices. Moreover, Labor does not have guidance on retaining specific documents for the grant award process and therefore cannot demonstrate that the grant award process has been conducted according to procedures.

Labor also provided technical comments that we incorporated as appropriate. State did not provide any technical comments.

Thomas Melito, Director
International Affairs and Trade

Appendix I: Objectives, Scope, and Methodology

This report reviews issues related to the Department of Labor's (Labor) Bureau of International Labor Affairs (ILAB) international technical assistance. The objectives of this report examined (1) how ILAB develops its technical assistance projects; (2) how ILAB selects recipients of its funding; and (3) how Labor manages its grant award documentation.

To describe how ILAB develops its technical assistance projects, we reviewed operations manuals of the Office of Child Labor, Forced Labor, and Human Trafficking (OCFT, referred to here as the child labor office) and the Office of Trade and Labor Affairs (OTLA, referred to here as the trade and labor office). These manuals contain chapters on project selection criteria, planning, and design. In addition, we reviewed ILAB's three annual reports on international child labor and forced labor: *Findings on the Worst Forms of Child Labor*; the *List of Goods Produced by Child Labor or Forced Labor*; and the *List of Products Produced by Forced or Indentured Child Labor*. We met with knowledgeable officials from the child labor and trade and labor offices to understand how they develop project ideas.

We also selected a nongeneralizable sample of 26 projects out of a total of 98 projects that were active in calendar years 2011, 2012, and 2013. To select this sample, we used lists of projects from fiscal years 2003 through 2012. These project lists are maintained by the child labor and trade and labor offices in ILAB. To determine the reliability of these lists, we met with the responsible officials and discussed how the lists are updated and maintained. We determined that these data were sufficiently reliable for the purposes of reporting ILAB's funding and selecting our sample of awards to review. We selected the sample based on several factors, such as dollar value and geographic location. The sample represents about 44 percent of ILAB funding over these years and includes 7 of the 9 grants with the highest dollar value ($10 million or above). Our sample includes projects that are single-country; multicountry; completed; ongoing; direct services; capacity building; and in most geographic regions. Because our sample is nongeneralizable, it cannot be used to make inferences about the population of ILAB grants.

To describe how ILAB selects recipients of its funding, we reviewed Labor guidance for the evaluation panels that review and assess the grant applications and the procurement office checklist for determining that applicants responded to the solicitation. We also met with knowledgeable officials from ILAB to discuss procedures for reviewing solicitations and evaluating applicants, the process for awards made using less than full and open competition, and steps ILAB takes to maximize competition. In addition, we met with grantees at their headquarters in Washington, D.C., and in Ecuador, Peru, Cambodia, and Thailand, to obtain their perspectives on the grant application process. We selected these locations based on, among other factors, size of grant, geographic location, and phase of the project.

To examine ILAB's management of grant award records, we developed a data collection instrument that we used to review the grant award files in our sample for key documents, including excluded parties list results,[1] Labor Procurement Review Board approval for less than full and open competition, panel evaluation worksheets for assessing competitive grant applications, and past performance information. We identified these documents based on ILAB policy documents such as guidance for the solicitation evaluation panels, the applicant evaluation worksheet template, and the solicitation for cooperative agreement template; OMB circular A-110; and interviews with Labor officials. In addition to the file review, we obtained and reviewed relevant documents such as Office of Procurement Service memos; the Department of Labor

Management Series chapter on grant and procurement management; the procurement office file checklist; and Retention and Access Requirements for Records, 29 C.F.R. § 97.42. We met with officials from ILAB and the Labor procurement office to discuss issues related to award file documentation. We used GAO's Standards for Internal Control in the Federal Government to assess Labor's grant award process including management of the award file documentation.[2]

We conducted this performance audit from June 2013 to May 2014 in accordance with generally accepted government auditing standards. Those standards require that we plan and perform the audit to obtain sufficient, appropriate evidence to provide a reasonable basis for our findings and conclusions based on our audit objectives. We believe that the evidence obtained provides a reasonable basis for our findings and conclusions based on our audit objectives.

APPENDIX II: ILAB CRITERIA FOR DEVELOPING NEW PROJECTS

The Office of Trade and Labor Affairs (trade and labor office) has several criteria for project development, including:

- Support for the broader foreign policy goals of the U.S. government as reflected in various trade legislation and other policy initiatives.
- Commitment by the stakeholders, including the government and workers' and employers' organizations, to protect the basic rights of workers and to the proposed project itself.
- Demonstrated need for technical assistance.
- Feasibility.
- Sustainability.
- Ability of the host government to absorb project resources.
- Ability to leverage additional support.
- Identification of a unique opportunity to provide resources that generate synergy and complement a national program or programs of other donor agencies.
- Anticipated risk.

The Office of Child Labor, Forced Labor, and Human Trafficking (child labor office) also has several criteria for project development, including:

- Nature and extent of exploitative child labor in a country.
- Contribution of proposed project to advancing the U.S. government's foreign policy objectives.
- Extent of a foreign government's acknowledgement of and commitment to eliminating the worst forms of child labor.
- Past performance of Labor-funded child labor projects in a given country.
- Presence and support of U.S. government field operations (i.e., U.S. embassies and the U.S. Agency for International Development).
- Likelihood that project interventions will have long-term and sustainable impact in reducing the incidence of exploitative child labor in the country.

End Notes

[1] On April 24, 2013, the Rana Plaza building collapsed in Dhaka, Bangladesh, killing over 1,100 factory workers and injuring many others.

[2] The International Labour Organization (ILO) is a tripartite U.N. agency with government, employer, and worker representatives. ILO's mission includes promoting fundamental rights at work, creating opportunities for decent employment and income, and enhancing social protection.

[3] A nongeneralizable sample seeks to systematically identify cases that will be useful for answering researchable questions. These selections may be either a nonprobability sample or a probability sample; however, results from a nongeneralizable sample cannot be used to make inferences about a population—in our case, the general population of ILAB assistance grants.

[4] These funds were subject to a 0.189 percent across-the-board rescission. Further Continuing Appropriations Act, 2013, Pub. L. No. 113-6, Div. F, § 1101. Additionally, ILAB reported that the fiscal year 2013 sequestration also affected ILAB's technical assistance funds.

[5] In fiscal year 2013, the worker rights office also obligated about $3.7 million from ILAB Salaries and Expenses—its operations funding account that can also be used for technical assistance—and about $3.4 million transferred from the State Department.

[6] This includes about $8.7 million from ILAB Salaries and Expenses used for technical assistance and $21 million that the State Department transferred to ILAB to fund projects.

[7] The United States has free trade agreements with 19 countries that include provisions to protect worker rights and facilitate cooperation among labor ministries. These labor provisions establish official processes for receiving complaints, or "submissions" from interested organizations that believe a trading partner is not fulfilling the labor commitments it made.

[8] ILAB publishes three annual reports on international child labor and forced labor: Findings on the Worst Forms of Child Labor; the List of Goods Produced by Child Labor or Forced Labor; and the List of Products Produced by Forced or Indentured Child Labor.

[9] According to ILAB officials, in some cases, it may not be possible for an ILAB grantee to fully implement a project without the support or at least official recognition of the host government. Lack of government support for a project can also undermine sustainability of the project. However, in some instances, ILAB may decide that the need for action in a country and the potential benefits that can be realized through a technical assistance project may justify moving forward even if host government support cannot be secured.

[10] We will be conducting a future review of ILAB's monitoring and evaluation, in which we will explore the extent to which ILAB collects evidence of sustainability and how it uses performance data to inform the design of future projects.

[11] According to ILAB officials, exploitative child labor includes those children (minors under age 18) working in the worst forms of child labor as outlined in ILO Convention 182 and children engaged in work that is exploitative and/or interferes with their ability to participate and complete required years of schooling, in line with ILO Convention 138.

[12] United States Department of Labor Bureau of International Labor Affairs, Findings on the Worst Forms of Child Labor, (Washington, D.C.: 2011, 2012).

[13] ILAB considers hazardous work to be work that is likely to harm the health, safety, or morals of children, such as work with dangerous machinery, equipment, and tools, or which involves the manual handling or transport of heavy loads.

[14] The System for Award Management is an online database that includes the excluded parties list system, among other federal procurement systems.

[15] An excluded party, subject to certain exceptions, is a person who is excluded by any federal agency and may not: (a) be a participant in certain federal agency transactions or (b) act as a principal of a person participating in one of those transactions. Transactions include grants, cooperative agreements, loans, and subsidies. 2 C.F.R. §§ 180.130 and 180.970.

[16] Panelists assign a numerical rating to each application based on the point values established in the solicitation. For example, the fiscal year 2012 solicitation for a child labor project in Ecuador and Panama stated the criteria and maximum point value for evaluating applications as follows: Project Design and Budget—60 points, Organizational Capacity—20 points, and Personnel and Project Management Plan—20 points.

[17] ILO received all but one of the noncompetitive grant awards, and received several of those through umbrella agreements. ILAB used these umbrella agreements when the agency received congressionally directed funding for ILO. Umbrella agreements are cooperative agreements covering funding for multiple individual projects implemented by one organization.

[18] Historically, ILO has received about half of ILAB's technical assistance funding for projects addressing worker rights and combating child labor. From 1995 through 1996, 1998 through 2006 and 2008 through 2010, Congress directed that ILAB use part of its appropriations for ILO projects to address child labor. Currently, because ILAB funds have not been congressionally-directed to ILO, ILO must compete for ILAB funding.

[19] Of the 14 competitive solicitations we reviewed, four award files lacked pre-award documents so we were not able to determine the number of applicants for those awards.

[20] The average funding amount for child labor grants from 2011 to 2013 is about $4.4 million, and the largest grant is $15 million. The average funding amount for trade and labor grants from 2011 to 2013 is about $1.5 million, and the largest grant is $10 million.

[21] According to ILAB officials, ILAB does not have its own grant office and relies on the procurement office in Labor's Office of the Assistance Secretary for Administration and Management for all of its grant office functions.

[22] Department of Labor, Office of Inspector General, Office of Audit, Department Oversight Needs to Be Strengthened to Minimize Procurement Risk, 17-12-002-07-711 (Washington, D.C.: Mar. 30, 2012).

[23] According to Labor officials, when Labor sends nonwinning applicants notification that they did not receive the award, applicants have 10 days to request a debriefing. After the debriefing, Labor destroys the documents associated with unsuccessful applications and only retains those of the winning applicant.

[24] Retention and Access Requirements for Records, 29 C.F.R. § 97.42.

[25] 29 C.F.R. § 97.42.

[26] GAO, Internal Control: Standards for Internal Control in the Federal Government, GAO/AIMD-00-21.3.1 (Washington, D.C.: November 1999).

End Notes for Appendix I

1 An excluded party, subject to certain exceptions, is a person who is excluded by any federal agency and may not: (a) be a participant in certain federal agency transactions or (b) act as a principal of a person participating in one of those transactions. Transactions include grants, cooperative agreements, loans, and subsidies. 2 C.F.R. §§ 180.130 and 180.970.

2 GAO, Internal Control: Standards for Internal Control in the Federal Government, GAO/AIMD-00-21.3.1 (Washington, D.C.: Nov. 1999).

In: International Labor Grants
Editor: Cristina M. Porter ISBN: 978-1-63482-398-2

Chapter 2

INTERNATIONAL LABOR GRANTS: DOL'S USE OF FINANCIAL AND PERFORMANCE MONITORING TOOLS NEEDS TO BE STRENGTHENED*

United States Government Accountability Office

WHY GAO DID THIS STUDY

According to the International Labour Organization, millions of children worldwide are engaged in labor that hinders their development. Recent incidents, including a factory collapse in Bangladesh, have highlighted poor working conditions overseas. ILAB's child labor office and trade and labor office provide funding to improve working conditions by supporting worker rights and combating child labor, mainly through international and nongovernmental organizations. The child labor office obligated about $56 million and the trade and labor office obligated about $13.5 million in fiscal year 2013. You asked us to review issues related to ILAB's international technical assistance. This report examines how ILAB (1) ensures the financial accountability of its technical assistance funds, (2) monitors the performance of its projects, and (3) evaluates its projects and uses the results of the

* This is an edited, reformatted and augmented version of a United States Government Accountability Office publication, No. GAO-14-832, dated September 2014.

evaluations. To address these objectives, GAO reviewed ILAB documents on financial requirements, performance monitoring, and evaluation. GAO analyzed a nongeneralizable sample of 26 grants that were active in calendar years 2011-2013. GAO selected this sample based on several factors, including dollar value and geographic location.

What GAO Recommends

GAO recommends that the Secretary of Labor take actions such as establishing guidance on time frames and criteria for accepting or rejecting financial reports, and implementing the trade and labor office's plans to conduct attestation engagements and develop common indicators. DOL agreed with GAO's recommendations.

What GAO Found

The Department of Labor's (DOL) Bureau of International Labor Affairs' (ILAB) child labor office and trade and labor office both have guidance for the financial monitoring of grants, but could improve their financial oversight. For example, we found that project managers completed their acceptance or rejection of about 20 percent of quarterly financial reports more than 90 days after receipt from the grantee, after the next quarter's report was due. ILAB does not have guidance that provides time frames and criteria for accepting or rejecting quarterly financial reports. In addition, although the child labor office supplements federal financial requirements with attestation engagements of selected projects to, among other things, assess the accuracy and reliability of grantee financial and performance data, the trade and labor office has not yet implemented its plan to conduct such attestation engagements of its grants, although officials said they plan to do so by November 2014. Without addressing these gaps in financial oversight, it could be difficult for ILAB to ensure federal resources are used efficiently and effectively to achieve desired objectives. The figure below outlines selected financial and performance monitoring tools and requirements from each office.

Monitoring	Child labor office	Trade and labor office
Financial	▪ ***Federal financial report: due each quarter***	▪ ***Federal financial report: due each quarter***
	Inventory list of all equipment and real property: ▪ ***Not specified for subgrantees***	Inventory list of all equipment and real property: ▪ ***Not specified for subgrantees***
Performance	Common indicators	▪ ***No common indicators***
Performance and financial	Attestation engagements: *for selected grants since 2005*	▪ ***No attestation engagements***

▪*Bolded text in Italics* indicates areas GAO identified for improvement.

Source: GAO analysis based on Department of Labor documenrs and officials. | GAO-14-832.

Financial and Performance Monitoring Tools and Requirements.

ILAB uses a number of tools to monitor the performance of its projects, but the trade and labor office's monitoring could be strengthened. Twenty-two of 26 grant files we reviewed included key monitoring documents, such as periodic performance progress reports. The child labor office requirements have generally been more comprehensive than those of the trade and labor office. For example, in contrast to the child labor office, the trade and labor office does not have common indicators that are used across projects and, as stated above, has not conducted attestation engagements of its grants. Without common indicators and attestation engagements, it is difficult for the trade and labor office to assess overall progress across projects and toward the office's goals, and whether its grantees are in compliance with relevant regulations.

ILAB conducts final evaluations for all projects to assess the performance of the project, including an assessment of performance against goals and objectives. Officials said they have drawn lessons learned from these evaluations that they have incorporated into subsequent projects, including addressing monitoring and evaluation issues earlier in a project. ILAB has also commissioned impact evaluations to determine whether a project has an effect and to quantify how large the effect is, and two have been completed to date.

ABBREVIATIONS

CMEP	comprehensive monitoring and evaluation plan
ILO	International Labour Organization
ILAB	Bureau of International Labor Affairs
DOL	Department of Labor
OCFT	Office of Child Labor, Forced Labor, and Human Trafficking
OTLA	Office of Trade and Labor Affairs

PMP	performance monitoring plan
TPR	technical progress report

* * *

September 24, 2014

The Honorable Orrin G. Hatch
Ranking Member
Committee on Finance United States Senate

The Honorable Lamar Alexander
Ranking Member
Committee on Health, Education, Labor and Pensions
United States Senate

According to the International Labour Organization (ILO),[1] millions of children worldwide are engaged in labor that hinders their education, development, and future livelihoods. In addition, recent incidents, including the collapse of a garment factory building in Bangladesh,[2] have highlighted poor working conditions overseas. In response to concerns about working conditions for children and adults, the U.S. government, in part through the Department of Labor's (DOL) Bureau of International Labor Affairs (ILAB), provides technical assistance mainly through international and nongovernmental organizations to improve working conditions by supporting worker rights and combating child labor.

You asked us to review issues related to ILAB's international technical assistance. This report examines how ILAB: (1) ensures the financial accountability of its technical assistance funds, (2) monitors the performance of its projects, and (3) evaluates its projects and uses the results of the evaluations. We issued a previous report examining ILAB's grant award process.[3]

To address these objectives, we reviewed relevant documents, including ILAB project manager manuals, management procedures and guidelines, a sample of grantee financial and technical progress reports, and project evaluations. We selected a nongeneralizable sample of 26 projects out of a total of 98 projects that were active in calendar years 2011, 2012, and 2013. [4] We selected the sample based on several factors, such as dollar value and geographic location. The sample represents about 44 percent of ILAB funding over these years and includes seven of the nine grants with the highest dollar value ($10 million or above). Our sample includes projects that are: single-country, multi-country, completed, on-going, direct services (such as education or livelihood support that the implementing organization provides directly to the targeted beneficiaries), capacity building, and in most geographic regions. We also discussed ILAB's processes for financial and performance monitoring, as well as evaluation of grants with officials from ILAB. In addition we discussed these processes with ILAB grantees in Washington, D.C., and during fieldwork in Cambodia, Ecuador, Peru, and Thailand. We selected these locations based on, among other factors, size of grant, geographic location, and phase of the project. To assess the reliability of the financial reports, we interviewed DOL officials about the E-grants system and asked about discrepancies we found during our review. We determined the data were sufficiently reliable for the purpose of determining the timeliness of acceptance of the financial reports and the amount of cash balances. To assess the reliability of the monitoring and project performance data, we verified the data in our sample by checking source documentation and followed up with ILAB to address any discrepancies. We determined that the data were sufficiently reliable for the purpose of reporting on compliance with monitoring requirements and project performance. Appendix I provides more information about our scope and methodology.

We conducted this performance audit from May 2014 to September 2014 in accordance with generally accepted government auditing standards. Those standards require that we plan and perform the audit to obtain sufficient, appropriate evidence to provide a reasonable basis for our findings and conclusions based on our audit objectives. We believe that the evidence obtained provides a reasonable basis for our findings and conclusions based on our audit objectives.

BACKGROUND

The mission of ILAB involves improving working conditions, promoting workers' rights, and addressing the workplace exploitation of children and other vulnerable populations overseas.

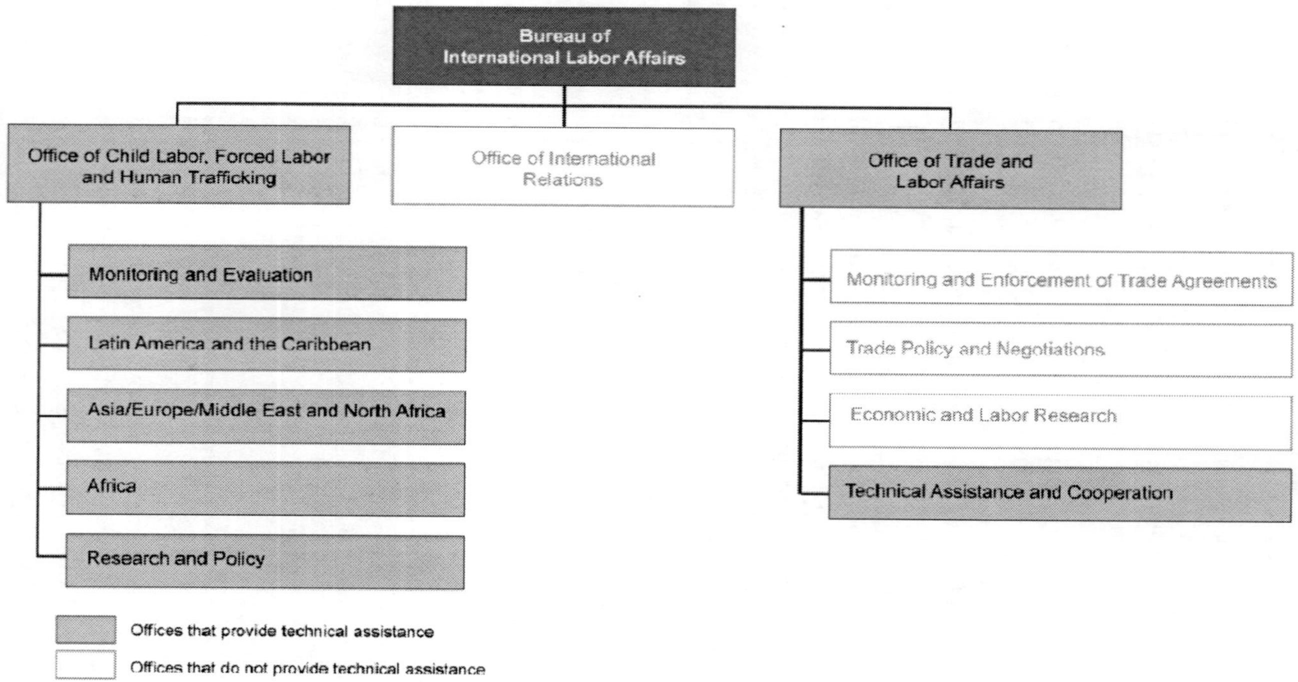

Source: Department of Labor. | GAO-14-832.

Figure 1. Bureau of International Labor Affairs Organization Chart with Offices That Provide Technical Assistance.

Objectives of the project included reducing child dropout rates, increasing the agricultural productivity of households with child laborers to reduce the use of child labor, and reducing hazardous labor among adolescents. During our visit to the project, we observed a school that had extended class hours to keep children in school in the afternoons to provide an alternative to working. In addition, the project provided the community a threshing machine so children no longer needed to separate grains from stalks by hand.

The trade and labor office's technical assistance focuses on projects to improve worker rights. According to the trade and labor office website, while there is no single definition or definitive list of workers' rights, ILO identifies what it calls "fundamental principles and rights at work" that all ILO members have an obligation to respect and promote, including freedom of association and the effective recognition of the right to collective bargaining, elimination of all forms of forced or compulsory labor, effective abolition of child labor, and elimination of discrimination in respect to employment and occupation. Additionally, according to DOL's website, United States trade law adds factors such as acceptable conditions of work with respect to minimum wages, hours of work, and occupational safety and health to that list, calling them "internationally recognized labor rights."

Workers around the world face unsafe working conditions, forced labor, long hours, workplace discrimination, and little or no right to representation or collective bargaining. In Peru, for example, indigenous communities are vulnerable to forced labor, including in the Amazon region, where indigenous adolescents and adults have been found under forced labor conditions, particularly in timber production and domestic service. Additionally, since 1991, Ukraine has experienced the second worst coal mine fatality rate in the world, with over 4,000 fatal accidents stemming from explosions and unsafe work conditions.

The trade and labor office funded 34 projects between fiscal years 2011 and 2013, including multicountry projects to advance worker rights and improve working conditions, such as the ILO Better Work program, which includes an independent monitoring system of garment factory conditions, as well as capacity building efforts targeting employers, workers and government officials. The trade and labor office has funded Better Work projects in several countries, including Cambodia and Haiti. For example, in fiscal year 2011, the trade and labor office provided $1 million to improve labor compliance in the footwear industry in Cambodia and to improve the capacity of labor law enforcement. Specifically, the project sought to address working conditions and improve the application of labor law and occupational health and safety regulations through training labor inspectors and providing capacity building and training to the Cambodian government to strengthen its capacity to govern the labor inspection system. During our visit to the project, we accompanied a project factory audit that included inspecting lighting, noise, and temperature levels in the factory; determining whether the factory conducted fire drills and provided access to first aid kits; and assessing the prevalence of sexual harassment.

ILAB Could Improve Its Processes for Financial Oversight

The child labor office and trade and labor office both have guidance for the financial monitoring of projects, but could improve their financial oversight. For example, we found that project managers completed their acceptance or rejection of about 20 percent of quarterly financial reports more than 90 days after receipt from the grantee, after the next quarter's report was due. ILAB does not have guidance that provides time frames and criteria for accepting or rejecting quarterly financial reports. In addition, although the child labor office supplements federal financial requirements with attestation engagements[12] of selected projects to, among other things, assess the accuracy and reliability of grantee financial and performance data, the trade and labor office has not yet implemented its plan to conduct such attestation engagements of its grants, although officials said they plan to do so by November 2014. Without addressing these gaps in financial oversight, it could be difficult for ILAB to ensure federal resources are used efficiently and effectively to achieve desired objectives.

ILAB Guidance Lacks Deadlines and Criteria for Accepting or Rejecting Quarterly Financial Report Review

Standard provisions generally in ILAB cooperative agreements and federal regulations require ILAB-funded grantees to submit quarterly federal financial reports no later than 30 days after the end of each quarter.[13] These grant-specific financial reports include information such as the grantee's cash receipts, expenditures, and on-hand cash balances.[14] Project managers said they use the financial reports, combined with other grantee information, to monitor the financial status of the project by comparing the rate of planned versus actual expenditures.

The child labor office has policies and guidance for project managers to review the grantee's quarterly financial report within 30 days after receipt. Officials said review could entail project managers' examining the report to ensure all required information is provided and following up with the grantee if there are any questions. The guidance requires project managers to accept the financial report in the DOL electronic grant management system to which the financial reports are submitted, called E-grants[15] and provide a written response by e-mail to the grantee, but the guidance does not specify a time frame in which the acceptance or rejection of documentation in E-grants is to occur, nor does it define circumstances in which project managers should accept or reject a report. According to officials, the project manager's review can take place without anything being recorded in E-grants, since E-grants records only the eventual formal acceptance or rejection of the quarterly financial report. According to officials, they do not want to reject a quarterly financial report for something that could be easily corrected, in part because rejecting the quarterly financial report can create delays for payments to the grantee. However, officials said that they can reject a financial report if they determine it is appropriate to do so. Child labor office officials told us that their staff who manage projects have an element in their performance standards related to meeting the 30-day review requirement.

Similarly, the trade and labor office also has policies and guidance for project managers to review the quarterly financial reports. According to the July 2013 trade and labor office guidance, project managers shall accept the financial report no later than 10 days after receipt if there are no issues with the report. If any discrepancies occur, according to the guidance, the project manager shall instead provide comments in E-grants and work with the grantee to address any issues prior to accepting the financial report. However, the guidance does not outline the circumstances in which project managers should reject a financial report. Officials told us that as of fiscal year 2014, project managers are now required to accept or reject the quarterly report no later than 30 days after receipt. According to trade and labor officials, the policy was revised in order to harmonize the standards with the child labor office and after determining there would not be a detrimental effect on the management of their projects. Trade and labor office officials also told us that their staff who manage projects have an element in their performance standards related to meeting this requirement.

In addition, ILAB's 2014 Operating Plan includes an indicator that reports the number of financial reports reviewed and processed. The indicator defines financial reports as reviewed and processed when accepted in E-grants. However, child labor officials said that project managers' quarterly reporting on the status of their review does not require that they formally accept the reports in E-grants. Child labor officials said that the data they report in the Operating Plan is based on the results of the project managers' quarterly report review. We found that, for the quarter ending June 30, 2013, this indicator in the operating plan included 2 reports from the child labor office that were not accepted in E-grants. Officials said they intend to amend the definition to measure the number of financial reports accepted or rejected (rather than reviewed and processed).

Our analysis of ILAB project managers' review of grantees' financial reports for the quarter ending June 30, 2013 showed that ILAB received 74 financial reports. We analyzed 71 financial reports for the timeliness of project manager review, as well as formal acceptance in E-grants.[16] Forty-three of these reports were for child labor office grants, and 28 were for trade and labor office grants. Child labor officials provided evidence that 12 of the 43 child labor office financial reports (about 28 percent) were reviewed within 30 days after receipt from the grantee, as described in the child labor office's policy manual (see table 1). Further, we found that 11 trade and labor financial reports (39 percent) were reviewed within 30 days after receipt from the grantee.[17]

Table 1. Percentage of Financial Reports Reviewed within 30 days after Grantee Submission

Child labor office	28% (12 of 43 reports)
Trade and labor office[a]	39% (11 of 28 reports)
Total ILAB	32% (23 of 71 reports)

Source: GAO analysis of Bureau of International Labor Affairs data. | GAO-14-832

[a]At the time the federal financial reports we reviewed were submitted, the trade and labor office required project managers to accept or reject them within 10 days. Since the trade and labor office has since changed its policy to 30 days, we assessed the office's review against the new policy.

Table 2 shows the percentage of quarterly financial reports ILAB project managers accepted in E-grants more than 90 days after the grantee's submission. We found that child labor office project managers accepted financial reports more than 90 days after the grantee's submission of the report in about 12 percent (5 reports) of the cases we reviewed. Trade and labor project managers accepted the financial reports more than 90 days after grantee submission in 32 percent (9 reports) of the cases we reviewed. Overall, we found that, for both offices in ILAB, 14 of the 71 financial reports we reviewed (about 20 percent) were accepted more than 90 days after receipt from the grantee.[18] In these cases, acceptance of the report was not completed before the next quarter's financial report was due. According to ILAB officials, the project manager's acceptance of 10 of these 14 reports was late because of the lack of adequate transition of responsibilities between project managers, as well as problems grantees and ILAB project managers had using E-grants, which officials said were outside their control.

Table 2. Percentage of Financial Reports Accepted More Than 90 days after Grantee Submission

Child labor office	12% (5 of 43 reports)
Trade and Labor office	32% (9 of 28 reports)
Total ILAB	20% (14 of 71 reports)

Source: GAO analysis of Bureau of International Labor Affairs data. | GAO-14-832

Standards for Internal Control in the Federal Government states that agency management is to develop policies, procedures, and practices that fit the agency's operations as it implements internal control standards.[19] In addition, for an entity to run and control its operations, it must have relevant, reliable, and timely communications relating to internal as well as external events. Pertinent information should be identified, captured, and distributed in a form and time frame that permits people to perform their duties efficiently. Without guidance on a time frame in which federal financial report review must be completed, including acceptance in E-grants, or guidance on criteria for accepting or rejecting a financial report in E-grants, it can be difficult for ILAB project managers to identify and address financial issues in a timely manner, and determine if federal funds are being used as intended.

Most Grantees Do Not Maintain Excess Federal Funds

Federal regulation requires that cash advances to a grantee be limited to the minimum amount needed and be timed to be in accordance with the actual, immediate cash requirements of the grantee in carrying out the purpose of the program. In addition, standard provisions generally in ILAB's cooperative agreements explain that advance payments to the ILAB-funded grantee are authorized provided that the grantee's financial management system meets certain requirements, including that the grantee have written procedures to minimize the time between the transfer of funds to the grantee and the grantee's payments for project expenses. Further, the standard provisions in ILAB's cooperative agreement template state that advances must be based on actual and immediate cash needs in order to minimize federal cash on hand in accordance with established policies.[20] ILAB officials told us that its project managers are responsible for monitoring excess cash[21] on hand as part of their review and acceptance of the financial report. According to ILAB officials, any concerns about excess cash require the project manager to follow up with the grantee.

As shown in table 3, we found that 47 out of 74 (over 60 percent) of the financial reports we reviewed did not show any federal cash on hand; however, 3 of the 74 financial reports had cash balances over $250,000. 22 ILAB officials told us that project managers noticed this excess during their review of the financial reports and contacted the grantees to correct the issues.

Table 3. Grantee Cash Balances Shown on Financial Reports for the Quarter Ending June 30, 2013

Amount of cash shown on financial report	Number of financial reports
None	47
Less than $250,000	24
Over $250,000	3

Source: GAO analysis of Bureau of International Labor Affairs data. | GAO-14-832

One grantee was responsible for two of the instances of excess cash balances over $250,000, specifically with balances of $806,160 and $870,000. According to ILAB officials, this grantee incorrectly transferred funds for other projects against these accounts. After the error was discovered, the grantee refunded the funds to these accounts. In the third instance, a grantee had a balance of approximately $263,000. Officials told us that they contacted the grantee, and the grantee responded that the balance was high because the grantee had not reconciled its accounts and had payments coming due, and would make the correction in the subsequent financial report. This grantee told us in September 2013 that it did not have written procedures for transferring cash from the federal payment management system to the grantee. These procedures could minimize the time between transfer of funds and payment of project expenses, as described by standard provisions generally found in ILAB's cooperative agreement. The grantee provided its written cash transfer procedures to ILAB in December 2013.

Child Labor Office Has Used Attestation Engagements to Monitor Grantees, while the Trade and Labor Office Is Planning Its First Engagement

The child labor office has contracted for over 40 attestation engagements since 2005, while the trade and labor office is planning its first engagement and is in the process of developing guidance to manage the engagements. Attestation engagements are a key control to ensure that grants are operating as intended. GAO's *Standards for Internal Control in the Federal Government* state that management is to implement control activities such as policies, procedures, techniques, and mechanisms needed to enforce its directives.[23]

The Child Labor Office Uses Attestation Engagements to Provide Additional Oversight of Cooperative Agreements

According to child labor office officials, to supplement federal government reporting requirements for grantees,[24] in 2005 they designed and began an attestation engagement program to provide additional financial and performance oversight of grantee activities. They engaged a certified public accounting firm to conduct attestation engagements of non-O:P grantees.[25] ILO projects are audited by ILO's designated external auditor.[26] During the period 2005–2013, 41 non-ILO projects were reviewed.

According to child labor office guidance, the purpose of these attestation engagements is to: (1) determine whether grantees are complying with the terms of their cooperative agreements and with DOL's regulations for grants,[27] (2) ensure that grantee financial reports are accurate and reliable, and (3) ensure that grantee performance data are accurate and reliable (performance will be discussed later in this report). The attestation engagement is divided into several broad areas, including the following:

- administrative procedures, internal controls, and fraud risk assessment;
- performance data, measures, and goals;

- budget;
- cash management;
- disbursements and financial reporting; and
- procurement and inventory management.

We reviewed the 7 attestation engagement reports issued between 2010 and 2013. These reports found 12 significant findings, 11 of which were related to performance issues, and 1 related to disbursements and financial reporting.[28] According to the attestation report, the significant financial finding was of discrepancies between the actual amounts an implementing organization paid to employees, teachers, and volunteers and the amounts charged to the project during the period of performance. Other financial-related findings in these attestation reports that resulted in recommendations include the late submission of quarterly federal financial reports and unsupported payroll costs.

The Trade and Labor Office Has Not Yet Conducted an Attestation Engagement or Developed Guidance to Manage Such Engagements

The trade and labor office's management procedures and guidelines state that all grantees are subject to attestation engagements (although it is not required), and at the time of our review, the trade and labor office had not engaged a contractor to perform attestation engagements. However, trade and labor office officials said they expect the first attestation engagement to take place by November 2014 after being delayed. In addition, at the time of our review, the trade and labor office had not yet developed official guidance for project managers to manage the attestation engagement. Attestation engagements are a key control that help ensure that cooperative agreements are operating as intended. GAO's *Standards for Internal Control in the Federal Government* states that control activities are the policies, procedures, techniques, and mechanisms that enforce management's directives.[29] In addition, these standards also call for continual monitoring and separate evaluations to assess the quality of performance over time.

In July 2014, trade and labor office officials said they were using the child labor office's existing contract agreement to finalize a task order[30] for the attestation contractor to conduct an attestation engagement and prepare guidance for future project managers to follow when utilizing attestation engagements to monitor their projects. They expect the guidance, which officials indicated will be similar to the child labor office's guidance, to take about 6 weeks to complete once the task order is awarded. ILAB officials plan to have the contractor use this guidance to carry out the first attestation engagement.

Without attestation engagements, the trade and labor office may not be able to determine whether grantees are in compliance with the terms of their agreements, ensure that financial reports are accurate and reliable, and ensure that performance data are accurate and reliable. Further, without guidance on managing these engagements, the trade and labor office may not be achieving the objectives of the attestation engagements.

Guidance for Reporting Subgrantee Inventory of Equipment and Real Property Needs Improvement

The child labor office and trade and labor office require grantees to report an inventory of all equipment and real property to DOL to comply with federal regulations on DOL grants.[31] Specifically, the guidance requires grantees to submit a list within 12 months of the award, at least once every 2 years, and as part of the closeout process.[32] Each office's guidance states that applicable provisions, including provisions in the cooperative agreement with the grantee, apply to the subgrantee. Standard provisions generally in ILAB's cooperative agreements state that grantees must follow DOL's policies in the acquisition, accounting for, and disposition of property. However, ILAB's guidance does not specifically state that the grantee's list include equipment and real property purchased by any subgrantees. For example, the child labor office's inventory list template included in its 2013 management procedures and guidelines does not refer to subgrantees. Officials stated that ILAB's legal and financial relationship is with the grantee, who is responsible for the subgrantee, including any inventory the subgrantee purchased with federal funds. ILAB officials said they would expect any subgrantee inventory to be included in the grantee's inventory list at closeout if the equipment was purchased using federal funds. GAO's *Standards for Internal Control in the Federal Government* states that agency management is to develop policies, procedures, and practices that fit the agency's operations as it implements internal control standards and that internal controls and all transactions need to be clearly documented.[33] Without specific guidance, it may not be clear whether grantees are including equipment and real property purchased by subgrantees. If the equipment and real property purchased by the subgrantees are not accurately reported by the grantee, there is a risk of a lack of accountability for assets purchased with DOL funds.

The Trade and Labor Office's Performance Monitoring Efforts Need Improvement

While ILAB uses a number of tools to monitor its grants, the child labor office requirements have generally been more comprehensive than those of the trade and labor office. For example, in contrast to the child labor office, the trade and labor office does not have common indicators that are used across projects to assess overall progress in key areas.[34] Grantees from both offices had difficulty meeting annual performance targets. Further, as stated above and again in contrast with the child labor office, the trade and labor office has not conducted attestation engagements of its grants. Without common indicators and attestation engagements, it is difficult for the trade and labor office to assess progress across projects and overall progress toward the office's goals, and whether its grantees are in compliance with relevant regulations. Finally, both offices use midterm evaluations, conducted at about the midpoint of a project's implementation, to make adjustments during the remainder of the project.

While the Child Labor Office Has More Comprehensive Performance Monitoring Requirements than the Trade and Labor Office, Both Offices Complied with Monitoring Requirements

The Child Labor Office Has More Comprehensive Monitoring Requirements than the Trade and Labor Office, Which Lacks Common Indicators and Attestation Engagements

The child labor office has monitoring requirements that the trade and labor office does not, including common indicators and attestation engagements. See figure 2 for a list of selected monitoring tools used by the child labor office and the trade and labor office.

The child labor office's monitoring system has evolved over the years and includes technical progress reports (TPR), a comprehensive monitoring and evaluation plan (CMEP) for direct services and capacity-building grants, and common indicators that are used across projects. The office also uses project-specific attestation engagements as mentioned previously to assess financial and performance issues. The requirements are described in the child labor office management procedures and guidelines.

Monitoring tool	Child labor office	Trade and labor office
Progress reports	• Status report—may be requested for two quarters per year, if deemed necessary by Department of Labor	• Status report—required two quarters per year (due January 30 and July 30)
	• Technical Progress Report—required every 6 months	• Technical Progress Report—required the other two quarters per year (due April 30 and October 30; more comprehensive than status reports)
Monitoring and evaluation plans	• Comprehensive Monitoring and Evaluation Plan—for grants with direct services to beneficiaries and/or capacity-building	• Not applicable
	• Performance Monitoring Plan—for non-direct services grants (e.g., for projects focused on policy, evaluation)	• Performance Monitoring Plan—for all grants—trade and labor grants generally do not provide direct services to individual beneficiaries
Baseline data[a]	• Baseline survey	• Baseline survey
■ Indicators and targets	■ *Common education and livelihood indicators and targets that are used across projects and project-specific indicators and targets*	■ *No common indicators*
	• Project-specific indicators and targets	• Project-specific indicators and targets
Evaluations	• Midterm and final evaluations	• Midterm and final evaluations
■ Attestation engagements	■ *Attestation engagements—for selected grants since 2005*	■ *No attestation engagements*

▪ *Text in Italics* indicates key differences between the offices' monitoring requirements.

Source: GAO analysis based on Department of Labor documents and officials. | GAO-14-832.

[a]Baseline data measure the existing conditions and provide information on the characteristics of the target population at the start of a project, including their living and working conditions.

Figure 2. Child Labor and Trade and Labor Offices' Selected Tools to Monitor Grantees.

Child labor office officials said that they emphasize the importance of monitoring and evaluation starting with the solicitation for applications. For fiscal year 2014 child labor office projects, solicitations require that about 8 percent of the grant award funding be used for monitoring and evaluation, according to officials. In addition, the monitoring and evaluation officer for the project is considered key project personnel so his/her qualifications are submitted with the grant application for ILAB's review.

The trade and labor office, which, according to officials, generally funds projects that have shorter timeframes and smaller budgets than those of the child labor office, has somewhat different monitoring requirements. The trade and labor office requirements include TPRs, a performance monitoring plan (PMP), and project-specific indicators. The requirements are described in the trade and labor office management procedures and guidelines.

Officials from the trade and labor office said that they are in the process of developing new monitoring initiatives, including using attestation engagements—to assess both financial and performance issues—and developing common indicators for selected grants. The trade and labor office's management procedures and guidelines state that all grantees are subject to attestation engagements, although they are not required. However, as stated above, the trade and labor office has not yet conducted any attestation engagements, although officials said they plan to conduct the first one by November 2014. Without attestation engagements, it is difficult for the trade and labor office to assess how well its grantees comply with DOL regulations and provisions of the cooperative agreement, as well as the reliability of the grantee's financial and performance reports.

Officials from the trade and labor office said that they currently do not have common indicators because the types of projects the office currently funds are different in nature than projects funded in previous years. For example, the office's current priority on strengthening the capacity of labor inspector governmental bodies is a new area for them. According to officials, the trade and labor office had common indicators in the past, but those indicators are not applicable to current projects, and they do not provide historical data on which to develop indicators that can be used across projects.[35] The Government Performance and Results Modernization Act requires agencies to report an update on agency performance including actual results in achieving performance goals for the 5 preceding years.[36] While the trade and labor office does include indicators in the agency's fiscal year 2013 annual performance report, including the number of countries in which worker rights and/or working conditions are improved, the report also states that the indicator does not accurately represent the scale of improvements that might be made in a country or group of countries, and that ILAB will refine the indicator in fiscal year 2014 to more accurately measure ILAB's work. According to trade and labor office officials, they are developing common indicators to better track progress over time. Without common indicators, it is difficult for the trade and labor office to assess overall progress toward its goals.

The Majority of Grant Files Included Required Monitoring Elements

Four (3 from the child labor office, 1 from the trade and labor office) of the 26 grant files we reviewed were missing one or more key monitoring elements, such as CMEPs or PMPs, baseline surveys, or indicator targets. [37] Twenty-two of the grants included the required monitoring elements.

- CMEP/PMP: 2 projects (from the child labor office) did not complete the required CMEP or PMP. According to officials, the CMEPs for these projects are in draft form. Both projects are scheduled to end in less than a year.
- Baseline survey: 1 trade and labor project in the Maldives and 1 child labor project in Pakistan did not have a baseline survey.
- Targets: 1 trade and labor office project in the Maldives did not have targets for the project's indicators.[38]

Officials from both offices told us they use additional means to monitor grants, including site visits, phone calls, and e-mails, since they do not have an overseas presence. Officials from the child labor office and trade and labor office said they also rely on other ILAB staff and embassy officials to meet with grantees when they make site visits. We found that 22 of 26 grants in our sample had received at least one site visit. Project managers try to visit at least twice during the life of the project for child labor grants, according to officials. Trade and labor officials said they prioritize site visits according to need and budget. Four grants in our sample had not had site visits at the time of our review. For example,

- Officials said they were not able to visit 1 project (Pakistan) because of security issues.
- ILAB officials said that manager for a project that began operating in 2013 in Cambodia, a site visit is planned for December 2014.

In our fieldwork countries, grantee officials stated that ILAB project managers are well informed and knowledgeable about the issues facing the projects. Grantee officials also said they have frequent communication with ILAB, and that ILAB project managers often have numerous comments on TPRs. Also during our fieldwork, we noted that U.S. embassy involvement in ILAB grants varied. For example, the labor officer in one of the embassies we visited in Asia was knowledgeable about ILAB projects in that country. In contrast, the labor officer in an embassy we visited in South America said there had been little information provided about a new ILAB project that was starting.

Grantees from Both Offices Had Difficulty Meeting Annual Performance Targets

According to child labor and trade and labor offices' guidance, performance indicators and their associated targets are required for monitoring project performance.[39] Officials from the child labor office said that they require potential grantees to submit life-of-project targets for the common indicators in their grant applications, and these targets then become part of the cooperative agreement. The child labor office's common indicators include the measurement of the provision of education and livelihood services.[40]

The child labor office also requires grantees to set annual fiscal year targets, including for the common indicators, to monitor project performance against overall life-of-project targets. Child labor office officials said that these annual targets can be modified, in consultation with ILAB, in the October TPR for the subsequent year.

For the most recent fiscal year, 2013, there were 9 active projects with common indicators in our sample that had fiscal year 2013 targets.[41] We analyzed 7 projects (see fig. 3).

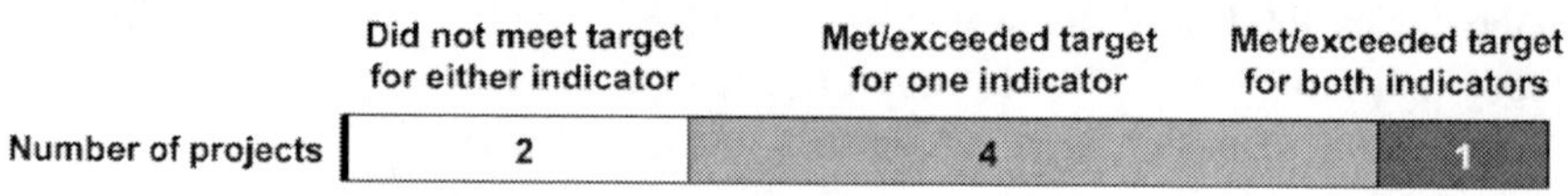

Source: GAO analysis of Bureau of International Labor Affairs data. | GAO-14-832.

Figure 3. Number of Child Labor Office Projects in Our Sample That Met or Exceeded Fiscal Year 2013 Common Indicator Targets.

Of these 7 projects, 1 project met or exceeded targets for both common indicators, 4 projects met or exceeded the target for one indicator, and 2 projects did not meet the target for either indicator. For the 4 projects that met or exceeded the target for one indicator, these projects achieved 74 to 92 percent of the target for the other indicator.

As discussed previously, the trade and labor office does not have common indicators, but requires projects to develop project-specific indicators and targets. According to trade and labor office officials, in 2013, the trade and labor office began requiring the Better Work country projects it funds to develop and submit semiannual performance monitoring plans with indicators, targets, and actual results. Officials said that these indicators and targets were developed by Better Work. Each project has numerous individual indicators and targets.

For the most recent project time period available (varying between the end of 2012 and the end of 2013), we counted the number of indicators with targets for each of 6 projects, determined for how many of those indicators the target was met or exceeded, and determined how many projects achieved various levels of success in meeting or exceeding their targets (see fig. 4).

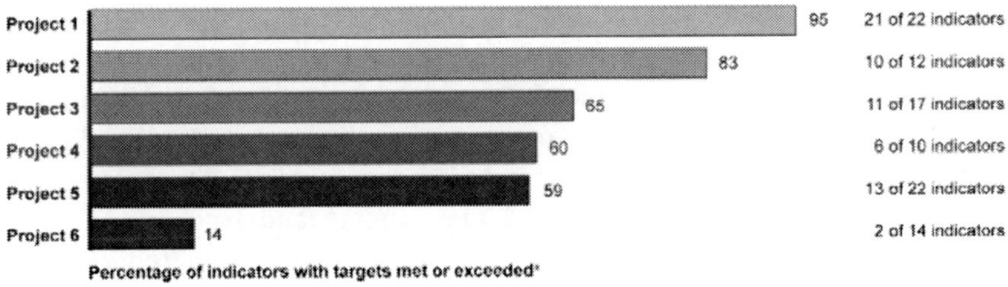

Source: GAO analysis of Bureau of International Labor Affairs data. | GAO-14-832.
[a]Only indicators with targets were included in this analysis.

Figure 4. Number of Trade and Labor Office Projects in Our Sample That Met or Exceeded Targets for Various Percentages of Indicators.

For 5 projects, the projects met or exceeded the targets for more than 50 percent of their indicators with targets. One project met or exceeded the targets for 14 percent of its indicators with targets, meaning it did not meet the targets for 86 percent.

A project could miss an annual target but still achieve its life-of-project targets, and there are many reasons why grantees might not achieve their targets, according to ILAB officials. For example, natural disasters or civil unrest are outside of the grantee's control and can result in a need to change project targets. However, projects can also miss their targets because of a flawed strategy that did not fully take into account the realities of the implementing environment. Child labor office officials said that they encourage grantees to set ambitious but realistic annual targets.

The Child Labor Office Uses Attestation Engagements and Both Offices Use Midterm Evaluations to Make Adjustments during the Remainder of the Project

Both offices hire independent contractors to conduct midterm project evaluations to assess project performance. Midterm evaluations for both offices and attestation engagements for the child labor office (which assess both financial and performance issues) identify areas for improvement during the second half of the project. We reviewed five child labor project midterm evaluations,[42] five trade and labor project midterm evaluations,[43] and seven child labor project attestation engagements to identify such improvements.[44]

The midterm evaluations and attestation engagements we reviewed found that ILAB projects are making progress toward goals, but identified areas for improvement. Evaluators and auditors highlighted several positive aspects of the projects. For example, auditors found that, in several projects, parents, teachers, and other community members were appreciative of the project and noted that children in the project are improving literacy skills and learning other new skills, and have stopped work or are working fewer hours. In addition, in Jordan, auditors reported that parents and teachers said that children were exhibiting fewer aggressive behaviors, and some children are gaining access to education for the first time. In Nicaragua and Indonesia, auditors found that awareness of exploitive child labor had increased in the target communities. The midterm evaluation of a Better Work project in Vietnam found that the project was likely to achieve its intended objectives, including strengthening the capacity of unions in export-oriented workplaces within the garment sector.

Evaluators and auditors also noted several areas for improvement, and ILAB officials responded. For example, project managers told us they use evaluations and attestation engagements as one way to have a check on source documentation that supports reported indicator results in TPRs because they do not and are not expected to examine source documentation, in part because it is not feasible for the material to be sent to Washington, D.C. Evaluators and auditors found cases in several projects where reported beneficiary data were not accurately supported. In addition, one attestation engagement we reviewed found that the project had misclassified beneficiaries because of incorrect understanding of the child labor office's definitions for children withdrawn or prevented from involvement with child labor. As a result, according to the attestation report, the project provided training to its staff so that they could correctly classify project beneficiaries to more accurately report the correct number of beneficiaries to the child labor office. Further, the midterm evaluation of a project in Jordan found that children were not able to participate in education activities because they lacked transportation. In response, the project began providing children with transportation. Midterm evaluations for three Better Work projects noted that the projects lack long-term sustainability. Trade and labor office officials acknowledged that sustainability takes a long time to achieve and much effort from stakeholders and funding from the host government. In response to a 2012 evaluation of the global Better Work program, DOL stated that it would like a better understanding of the role that host country governments will play in either the general sustainability aspect of Better Work or in the specific area of enforcement, and how that government's role ties into the future vision for the program. Trade and labor office officials said that while ILO's approach to sustainability has been focused on cost recovery and financing of the Better Work program itself, trade and labor office officials said they have a broader view about what sustainability can mean. For example, training and improving the capacity of government labor inspectors so that a Better Work project is not needed is a form of sustainability. Updates on project activities in response to evaluation and attestation engagement recommendations are also included in TPRs, as relevant.

FINAL PROJECT EVALUATIONS HAVE INFORMED CHANGES TO CHILD LABOR PROJECTS, BUT MOST IMPACT EVALUATIONS ARE NOT YET COMPLETE

ILAB officials said they have drawn lessons learned from final project evaluations that assess performance against goals and objectives, but it is too early to determine the usefulness of impact evaluations. The child labor office and trade and labor office both require final evaluations for all completed projects and have general guidance for disseminating the evaluation results to inform new projects. Project evaluations, such as the midterm and final evaluations, are assessments of performance against goals and objectives. They are used to answer questions about design, implementation, and results.

The final evaluations identify project achievements as well as cross-cutting areas for improvement. Child labor office officials said they have drawn some lessons learned from the evaluations that they have incorporated into subsequent projects, including addressing monitoring and evaluation issues earlier in a project. Impact evaluations, in contrast to project evaluations, seek to answer cause-and-effect questions. Their purpose is to determine whether a program has an impact and to quantify how large the impact is. Because only two impact evaluations have been conducted to date for the child labor office, it is too early to determine the usefulness of their results. Officials from the trade and labor office said that they had not previously had dedicated funding to conduct impact evaluations, but are planning to start them with funding assistance from DOL's Chief Evaluation Office.

Final Project Evaluations Underline Positive Effects as well as Cross-cutting Weaknesses

As with the midterm evaluations, the child labor office and the trade and labor office hire independent contractors to carry out final project evaluations to assess project performance. These evaluations are assessments of performance against goals and objectives. They are used to answer questions about design, implementation, and results. According to ILAB guidance, the final project evaluation is a key tool that helps both offices better prepare for new projects because evaluation findings are used for planning future projects. The child labor office requires a final evaluation no later than 3 months before the end of a project; the trade and labor office requires the final evaluation to take place at least 4 to 6 months prior to the end of the project period. Exceptions to these rules are allowed on a case-by-case basis. Both offices in ILAB have guidance about procedures project managers and independent evaluators need to follow. For example, the terms of reference for the evaluation specify key areas of focus that a final evaluation needs to cover, such as relevance, effectiveness, efficiency, and sustainability.

Final evaluations make recommendations to grantees and ILAB for improvement. In our sample of 26 projects covering both offices, there were 8 completed projects, all of which were funded by the child labor office between fiscal year 2006 and fiscal year 2013.[45] Of these 8, 1 did not have a final evaluation on file. Although the grantee of this project commissioned a contractor to perform the final evaluation, the child labor office could not accept the report because of its poor quality, according to officials.[46]

The evaluations found that the projects were generally relevant to the local context and supported the main goals of DOL. Projects also had positive effects on raising awareness of child labor issues and, in some cases, empowering communities. However, our analysis of the evaluations found the following cross-cutting areas of weakness—issues with data, livelihoods and other support services, and project staffing— with potential consequences for project effectiveness and sustainability:

- *Data concerns:* In 3 projects, the number of children withdrawn and prevented from involvement with child labor were not always counted or targeted in a consistent manner. In 2 projects, an emphasis on achieving preset numerical targets raised evaluators' concerns about the quality of services delivered. Child labor officials told us establishing targets is a balancing act. For example, setting targets too low and ending up with final numbers far in excess of targets could also indicate flaws in project design.[47]
- *Weaknesses in livelihoods and other support services:* Four of the final evaluations we reviewed found that vocational or skill training programs were not always appropriate, either because they were too short in duration, did not provide the beneficiaries the necessary tools, or lacked local labor market research, which could have secured beneficiary children apprenticeships and practical training with local employers. In addition, the evaluations of three projects found support could be strengthened for family livelihood and income generation activities to tackle the root causes of child labor, including household poverty and lack of educational opportunities. Further, four of the evaluations we reviewed recommended adding psychosocial support for beneficiary children.[48]
- *Staffing concerns:* Staff problems in projects, such as high turnover rates, low pay, varying degrees of skill, and workload were raised in 4 final evaluations. One project experienced delays because the host government instituted a requirement that the project's country director be a host country national, and as a result, would not grant a visa to the foreign-national director hired by the grantee.

In addition, to inform staff of recurring themes across project evaluations, the child labor office commissioned a synthesis report in 2012 that systematically reviewed the findings of 48 final project evaluations. The report found that projects generally met ILAB's goals, such as achieving targets for withdrawing and preventing children from child labor, and increasing awareness about the importance of education for all children. The report also points to promising activities that were implemented across several countries, including well-conducted remedial classes and early-childhood development initiatives. However, the report found that the goal of ensuring the long-term sustainability of activities was not always achieved, mainly because recipient countries generally lack the necessary resources.

ILAB Has Drawn Lessons Learned from Project Evaluations

Both the child labor office and the trade and labor office have guidance stating that one of the roles of project managers is to ensure that the office is applying learning from evaluations and feeding knowledge back into new and ongoing projects, as appropriate. Child labor officials told us they make adjustments to projects and strengthen processes based on evaluation recommendations, as needed. For example, the office anticipates fewer data quality issues with recent projects because the new CMEP process, which all new direct beneficiary projects have had to implement since fiscal year 2012, requires grantees to focus on data collection and reporting early in the project. Child labor officials also said they now require grantees to assess local labor market conditions, if they include vocational training in their project proposals, to ensure there is demand for the skills they plan to teach. For example, a 2013 solicitation for a project in Morocco states that applicants' strategies must be based on labor market research to ensure that the services available through the project are linked with local employment options. In addition, the fiscal year 2010 appropriations conference report directed that funds may be used to support livelihood assistance activities as part of projects,[49] which officials said addresses some of the issues about family livelihoods that evaluators raised in the past. Child labor officials also told us they strongly encourage grantees to hire local nationals as key personnel for their projects to satisfy potential host government requirements and avoid delays in project start, as well as build local capacity.

To disseminate the results of evaluations and their related lessons, the child labor office keeps an internal electronic repository of project evaluations organized by country, region, and topic, which staff can consult when scoping projects, according to officials. Child labor officials said they do not currently plan to produce more of the synthesis reports of evaluations, relying instead on the repository.

Similarly, the trade and labor office's guidance lists steps project managers should follow to disseminate evaluation findings, including briefing interested parties in DOL within 2 weeks and sharing the report and its findings with all relevant stakeholders. Officials from the trade and labor office said all evaluations are on a shared drive accessible to project managers. ILAB officials also told us project managers share the findings and recommendations of evaluations in informal meetings.

In addition, external stakeholders can find evaluations on ILAB's website, which makes publicly available most midterm and final evaluations of projects. DOL is in the process of uploading more evaluations, officials told us, as part of website improvements. It aims to have all evaluations available on its website. Two grantees we spoke to said that they used project evaluations from ILAB's website to help them develop their grant proposals. One project manager also said that she encourages grantees to review these evaluations to see if they have lessons that are applicable for the grantees' projects.

While ILAB Has Funded Impact Evaluations of Selected Components of Projects, Most Remain Incomplete, Making the Usefulness of Their Results Difficult to Determine

In addition to final project evaluations, since 2008, the child labor office has provided funding to several organizations to carry out impact evaluations of specific activities in 7 projects.[50] Two of these are complete. Unlike project evaluations, ILAB does not require impact evaluations, but conducts them to obtain information on what types of interventions are effective in reducing child labor and can be used as the basis for replicating successful activities.

Impact evaluations seek to answer cause-and-effect questions. Their purpose is to determine whether a program has an impact and to quantify how large the impact is. For example, impact evaluations often involve randomly assigning eligible individuals or children to two groups, one of which participates in the program or activity that is being evaluated (treatment group), while the other does not (control group). The random assignment ensures that the two groups are statistically the same, and any difference seen later can be attributed to one group having participated in the program and the other not. Thus, impact evaluations measure program effectiveness typically by comparing the outcomes of the two groups.

So far, two impact evaluations have been completed. Three are still ongoing, and two have been halted, largely because of concerns about data quality, as well as delays and deviations from original implementation plans, which would potentially skew results, according to officials.

The child labor office considered a number of factors when selecting projects for impact evaluation, according to officials, including the size of the population served by the project; the implementing environment— whether the country was stable and receptive to the idea of an impact evaluation, as not all countries are—and whether the project included livelihood services. In 2013, the child labor office held a workshop for impact evaluation implementers to share lessons learned from their experience and report on progress.

One impact evaluation found that an extended-hours school activity in Bolivia had mixed effects on the school or work situation of beneficiary children, possibly increasing school enrollment among rural children while decreasing it among urban children. The evaluation also found no impact on participation in hazardous child labor. The other completed impact evaluation, of a project combating child labor through education and livelihood support in Egypt, found that the project had a significant positive impact on school enrollment, attendance, and time spent on school-related activities, especially for girls and young children. It also found that the amount of time beneficiary children were working had been reduced, but no evidence that the education project had an impact on the children's overall participation in work, or their exposure to workplace hazards, suggesting that the intervention may need to be reformulated to reach the ultimate objective of withdrawing and preventing children from involvement in hazardous child labor.

In 2006, the child labor office also funded ILO to undertake six tracer studies, as part of the broader work on impact assessment, with an expected delivery date in 2011. Tracer studies look back at a sample of children who have already been provided educational services and present evidence on the extent to which such interventions have longterm effect on the lives of beneficiary children. ILO has supplied only four tracer studies to date, two of which are not available in English.[51]

Because there are only two completed impact evaluations, both of which were carried out in 2013, out of the seven that have been funded by the child labor office since 2008, it is too early to gauge how the office will use them to inform future project design. As indicated earlier, the two impact evaluations conducted so far suggest that the education projects likely need modifications to have a significant effect on withdrawing and preventing children from participating in child labor. Similarly, since only four of the six tracer studies commissioned in 2006 were delivered, it is unclear how the tracer studies will inform future project design for the child labor office, especially when a language barrier limits their wide dissemination.

Trade and labor officials said that in the past, the office did not have dedicated funding to commission impact evaluations of their projects but that they have recently begun one with financial assistance from DOL's Chief Evaluation Office for that purpose. However, they noted that this assistance is not guaranteed in future years. According to officials, lack of funding is a real constraint given that the cost of evaluation is high compared with the cost of projects. For example, an impact evaluation currently under way of a worker rights project in Colombia cost about $950,000, which is over 60 percent of the project cost. Trade and labor officials told us the Colombia project was selected because similar projects are being considered in other Central American countries, so finding out about the impact of the project is important. Until recently, most of the trade and labor office's largest grants have been directed towards the Better Work projects implemented by ILO, and ILO has commissioned an impact evaluation of these projects. Because DOL is not providing funding for this effort, the trade and labor office officials told us that it has access only to reports and data that ILO makes publicly available.[52]

CONCLUSION

Congress funds the child labor and trade and labor offices to, among other things, combat exploitative child labor internationally and implement model programs that address worker rights issues. These funds are used to address the conditions that could lead to disasters such as the factory collapse in Bangladesh and the tragedy of millions of children around the world facing harsh employment conditions and missing out on educational opportunities. DOL project managers use many tools to monitor whether projects are on track to meet objectives, but improving use of some of these tools could help DOL achieve its goals for the projects it oversees.

Project managers use the quarterly financial report to ascertain how projects are managing their funds; however, ILAB guidance lacks deadlines and criteria for when quarterly financial reports must be formally accepted or rejected. For about 20 percent of the reports we reviewed, project managers did not formally accept them in DOL's electronic grant management system until after the next quarter's reports were due. This can make it difficult to identify and address financial issues in a timely way.

- Because of a lack of specific guidance, grantees may not be clear about requirements to ensure that submitted inventory lists include inventory lists of subgrantees. If the equipment and real property purchased by the subgrantees are not accurately reported by the grantee, there is a risk of a lack of accountability for assets purchased with DOL funds.
- Attestation engagements can be key to ensuring that grants are operating as intended. Although the child labor office uses attestation engagements, the trade and labor office to date has not used them, although it plans to by November 2014. Without attestation engagements, it is difficult for the trade and labor office to assess how well its grantees comply with DOL regulations and provisions of the cooperative agreement, as well as the reliability of the grantees' financial and performance reports.
- While the trade and labor office has project-specific indicators to measure the progress of individual grants, it lacks a way to assess performance across all of its grants. Without common indicators, it is difficult for the trade and labor office to assess overall progress toward its goals.

Financial and performance monitoring tools are key to ensuring that federal funds are used as intended and that programs are as effective as possible. Without improved oversight, these programs are at increased risk of not meeting the goals of improving working conditions, protecting workers' ability to exercise their rights, and addressing the workplace exploitation of children and other vulnerable populations.

RECOMMENDATIONS FOR EXECUTIVE ACTION

To improve ILAB's financial and performance monitoring, we recommend that the Secretary of Labor, in concert with ILAB management, take four actions:

1) to facilitate the effective financial oversight of its grants, establish guidance specifying time frames in which project managers must

accept or reject quarterly financial reports and the criteria for accepting or rejecting the reports;

2) to better ensure accurate accounting of federal funds, revise ILAB policies to specify that subgrantee inventories of equipment and real property purchased with federal funds are included in inventory lists submitted by the grantee;
3) to improve financial and performance monitoring of trade and labor grants, implement the trade and labor office's plan to conduct attestation engagements and develop guidance on the management of these engagements; and
4) to improve performance monitoring of trade and labor grants, ensure that the trade and labor office implement its plan to develop common indicators to track progress across projects.

AGENCY COMMENTS AND OUR EVALUATION

We provided a draft of this report to DOL for comment. We also provided relevant sections to the State Department for technical comment.

In its written comments, DOL stated that it agreed with GAO's recommendations to improve their financial and performance monitoring. Specifically, DOL reported that the child labor office is incorporating into its operation manual the same standard that the trade and labor office has recently established—which is for project managers to accept or reject quarterly financial reports within 30 days after the reports are due. In addition, DOL said that it will translate its informal guidance and standards for accepting or rejecting financial reports into formal written criteria. DOL also stated that it has taken measures to revise the language in ILAB's cooperative agreements and management procedures and guidelines to specify that grantee inventory reporting requirements must include items purchased by subgrantees. Further, DOL explained that the trade and labor office has initiated the planning process for its first attestation engagement, including development of guidance for managing these engagements. Finally, DOL said that the trade and labor office is including six new common indicators in ILAB's internal fiscal year 2015 operating plan. DOL and the State Department also provided technical comments, which we incorporated as appropriate.

Thomas Melito, Director
International Affairs and Trade

APPENDIX I: OBJECTIVES, SCOPE, AND METHODOLOGY

This report reviews issues related to the Department of Labor's (DOL) Bureau of International Labor Affairs (ILAB) international technical assistance. The objectives of this report examined how ILAB: (1) ensures the financial accountability of its technical assistance funds, (2) monitors the performance of its projects, and (3) evaluates its projects and uses the results of the evaluations.

To assess how ILAB ensures the financial accountability of its technical assistance funds, we reviewed ILAB management procedures and guidelines and operations manuals of the child labor office and the trade and labor office. These manuals contain chapters on cooperative agreements and procedures for audits of technical assistance programs. We also reviewed the ILAB cooperative agreement template and attestation engagement reports. To determine whether ILAB project managers are following ILAB's guidance regarding timely review of quarterly financial reports, we selected the entire population of 74 financial reports submitted to ILAB for the quarter ending June 30, 2013. We selected the quarter ending June 30, 2013 on a nonprobability basis. We compared the date the grantee certified the financial report with the date ILAB project managers accepted it to determine whether the project manager was in compliance with ILAB's guidance. Further, we analyzed the financial reports to determine the amount of cash the grantee reported as of June 30, 2013. To assess the reliability of the financial reports, we interviewed DOL officials about the E-grants system and asked about discrepancies we found during our review. We determined the data were sufficiently reliable for the purpose of determining the timeliness of acceptance of the financial reports and the amount of cash balances. In addition, we interviewed ILAB officials to understand the processes for financial monitoring of cooperative agreements. To the extent necessary, we compared the information obtained with GAO's *Standards for Internal Control in the Federal Government.*[1]

We selected a nongeneralizable sample of 26 projects out of a total of 98 projects that were active in calendar years 2011, 2012, and 2013. To select this sample, we used lists of projects from fiscal years 2003 through 2012. These project lists are maintained by the child labor and trade and labor offices in ILAB. To determine the reliability of these lists, we met with the responsible officials and discussed how the lists are updated and maintained. We determined that these data were sufficiently reliable for the purposes of reporting ILAB's funding and selecting our sample of awards to review. We selected the sample based on several factors, such as dollar value and geographic location. The sample represents about 44 percent of ILAB funding over these years and includes seven of the nine grants with the highest dollar value ($10 million or above). Our sample includes projects that are single-country, multicountry, completed, ongoing, direct services (such as education or livelihood support that the implementing organization provides directly to the targeted beneficiaries), capacity building, and in most geographic regions. Because our sample is nongeneralizable, it cannot be used to make inferences about the population of ILAB grants.

To examine how ILAB monitors the performance of its projects, we reviewed ILAB monitoring guidance, including management procedures and guidelines and operations manuals of the child labor office and trade and labor office. These manuals contain chapters on technical assistance/cooperative agreements, project administration, project oversight, and monitoring and evaluation. We developed a data collection instrument to assess the compliance of the 26 grants in our sample with selected monitoring requirements, such as technical progress reports, monitoring plans, and site visit reports. We identified these requirements based on ILAB guidance documents, including the management procedures and guidelines and the operations manuals from both the child labor office and the trade and labor office. One analyst completed the data collection instrument and another analyst verified the entries. In addition, we interviewed ILAB officials about any questions related to the data. To assess the extent to which the 12 active child labor projects in our sample achieved fiscal year 2013 targets for the child labor office's two common indicators, we used the office's indicator tracking sheet. To assess the reliability of the data in the tracking sheet, we used the actual results and fiscal year 2013 targets reported in each project's October 2013 technical progress report. For 8 projects, we identified discrepancies between the tracking sheet and the technical progress reports. ILAB provided additional supporting documentation to resolve the discrepancies for 6 of those 8 projects and indicated that it was working with the grantees for the other 2 projects to clarify the data they had reported. We excluded these 2 projects from our analysis. We also excluded 3 projects that did not have fiscal year 2013 targets, leaving a total of 7 projects in our analysis. In addition, since the trade and labor office does not have common indicators used across all projects, we counted the number of indicators with targets for each of 6 ongoing trade and labor projects Better Work country projects in our sample and analyzed how many of those targets the project met or exceeded for the most recent project time period available (varying between the end of 2012 and the end of 2013).[2] We pulled the indicator targets and results data from the data-tracking tables provided by these projects to ILAB. To assess the reliability of the data, we met with trade and labor officials to discuss how they verify grantee data. According to officials, the grantee is responsible for the accuracy of the data, and data quality is checked through audits and evaluations. However, the ILAB project manager does not engage in ongoing data validity checks. We determined that the data were sufficiently reliable for the purpose of reporting on compliance with monitoring requirements and project performance for the projects in our sample. We also met with knowledgeable officials from ILAB, including 11 project managers, to discuss how they provide oversight of their grants. In addition, we met with grantees at their headquarters in Washington, D.C., and in Ecuador, Peru, Cambodia, and Thailand, to obtain their perspectives on how ILAB monitors grants. We selected these locations based on, among other factors, size of grant, geographic location, and phase of the project.

To examine how ILAB evaluates its projects and uses the results of its evaluations, we reviewed seven final evaluations for the completed child labor projects in our sample 3 and the two completed impact evaluations ILAB had conducted. We discussed the completed final evaluations and impact evaluations with ILAB officials, including project managers responsible for the projects, to discuss the evaluation findings and how ILAB used those findings. We also discussed ongoing impact evaluation efforts.

We conducted this performance audit from May 2014 to September 2014 in accordance with generally accepted government auditing standards. Those standards require that we plan and perform the audit to obtain sufficient, appropriate evidence to provide a reasonable basis for our findings and conclusions based on our audit objectives. We believe that the evidence obtained provides a reasonable basis for our findings and conclusions based on our audit objectives.

End Notes

[1] The International Labour Organization (ILO) is a tripartite UN agency with government, employer, and worker representatives. ILO's mission includes promoting fundamental rights at work, creating opportunities for decent employment and income, and enhancing social protection.

[2] On April 24, 2013, the Rana Plaza building collapsed in Dhaka, Bangladesh, killing over 1,100 factory workers and injuring many others.

[3]GAO, *International Labor Grants: Labor Should Improve Management of Key Award Documentation*, GAO-14-493 (Washington, D.C.: May 2014).

[4] A nongeneralizable sample seeks to systematically identify cases that will be useful for answering researchable questions. These selections may be either a nonprobability sample or a probability sample; however, results from a nongeneralizable sample cannot be used to make inferences about a population-–in our case, the general population of ILAB assistance grants.

[5] Further Continuing Appropriations Act, 2013, Pub. L. No. 113-6, Div. F, § 1101. Pursuant to section 1101, fiscal year 2013 funds were made available to ILAB to the extent and in the manner that was provided by the prior year appropriations act: Consolidated Appropriations Act, 2012. Pub. L. No. 112-74, 125 Stat. 786, 1061. For fiscal year 2013, these funds were subject to a 0.189 percent across-the-board rescission. Additionally, ILAB reported that the fiscal year 2013 sequestration also affected ILAB's technical assistance funds.

[6] In fiscal year 2013, the trade and labor office also obligated about $3.7 million from ILAB Salaries and Expenses—its operations funding account that can also be used for technical assistance—and about $3.4 million transferred from the State Department.

[7] ILAB funded 74 grants from 2011 to 2013. The average funding amount for child labor grants from 2011 to 2013 was about $4.4 million, and the largest grant was $15 million. The average funding amount for trade and labor grants from 2011 to 2013 was about $1.5 million, and the largest grant was $10 million.

[8] This includes about $8.7 million from ILAB Salaries and Expenses used for technical assistance and $21 million that the State Department transferred to ILAB to fund projects.

[9] An ILO convention is a legally binding international treaty which may be ratified by member states, according to ILO. ILO's governing body has identified eight conventions as "fundamental", covering subjects that are considered as fundamental principles and rights at work, which includes Convention 182 on the worst forms of child labor. ILO Convention 182 has been ratified by 179 countries, including the United States.

[10] For the purpose of this report, we refer to such types of work as hazardous work.

[11] Examples of non-hazardous work could include performing household chores that do not expose children to dangerous activities, assisting parents in a family business outside of school hours, and working in non-hazardous activities after school or during vacations to earn extra income.

[12] In an attestation engagement, a certified independent public accountant may assess a broad range of financial and performance subjects and report on the results.

[13] For quarterly reports, DOL's *"Financial Reporting*" regulation requires grant recipients to submit to DOL financial reports no later than 30 days after the end of the quarter. 29 C.F.R. § 95.52 (a)(1)(iv).

[14] Cash balances are the amount of cash the grantee has drawn down from its project account in the Department of Health and Human Services payment management system in excess of the grantee's current cash expenditures. Grantees request cash advances using the Department of Health and Human Services payment management system to meet their immediate cash needs.

[15] E-grants is DOL's grant management system which integrates four existing systems used in the grant process: (1) E-procurement system; (2) Grants.gov; (3) New Core Financial Management System; and (4) Department of Health and Human Services payment management system.

[16] Of the 74 reports submitted to ILAB, we excluded 3 from our analysis of ILAB review and acceptance of the financial reports because we could not verify their acceptance dates in E-

grants and 1 was not accepted in E-grants. ILAB told us that it is researching 2 to determine the correct ILAB acceptance dates. In addition, 1 report has not been accepted because ILAB has outstanding questions with the grantee.

[17] According to officials, ILAB considers the date of receipt of financial reports to be the due date for all reports in a given financial quarter, which would be 30 days after the end of the financial period in question. For example, this would mean July 30 for the financial quarter ending June 30. This would give project managers until August 29 to review the financial report, regardless of whether the grantee submitted the report prior to July 30. Against this broader application of the policy, we found that child labor project managers reviewed 18 of 43 financial reports (42 percent) within 30 days of the grantee's submission deadline. Trade and labor project managers reviewed 11 of 28 financial reports (39 percent) within 30 days of the grantee's submission deadline.

[18] We were unable to determine whether any of the financial reports in our sample had been rejected. According to officials, rejecting a financial report from E-grants allows the grantee to make changes to the report. Once the grantee re-submits the report, E-grants does not allow a user to identify that it had been previously rejected.

[19] GAO, *Standards for Internal Control in the Federal Government*, GAO/AIMD-00-21.3.1 (Washington, D.C.: Nov. 1999). Section 3512 (c) and (d) of Title 31 of the United States Code (commonly known as the Federal Managers' Financial Integrity Act (FMFIA)) requires the Comptroller General to issue standards for internal control in government. These standards, known as the Standards for Internal Control in the Federal Government (Green Book), provide the overall framework for establishing and maintaining an effective internal control system.

[20] According to the template, these policies are established in Treasury Department Circular 1075 and 29 C.F.R. part 95.

[21] For the purposes of this report, we use the term excess cash to refer to cash balances that are in excess of the grantee's current cash expenditures.

[22] We determined that these 3 grants represent over 70 percent of total cash on hand. In addition, 24 grants had less than $250,000 cash on hand, with balances ranging from $1,825 to $121,141.

[23] GAO/AIMD-00-21.3.1.

[24] Prior to December 26, 2013, all nonfederal entities that expend $500,000 or more of federal awards in a year were required to obtain an annual audit in accordance with the Single Audit Act (single audit), as amended 31 U.S.C. Ch. 75. Subsequent to December 26, 2013, entities must expend $750,000 or more before a single audit is required. Single audits are focused on recipients' internal controls over financial reporting and compliance with laws and regulations governing U.S. federal awardees and provide key information about the federal grant's financial management and reporting. We reviewed 12 grantees' single audits, of which 11 had clean opinions. We found one issue regarding the child labor office's compliance with procedures and another technical issue related to a trade and labor grant that is primarily a DOL Office of Inspector General responsibility. Further, we noted that ILAB grants are generally not considered major programs and are not the subject of a single audit for a particular recipient of federal funds.

[25] The child labor office has a written methodology to select grantees for attestation engagements based on an assessment of the risk that the grantee may not be complying with regulations and cooperative agreement provisions, or not submitting reliable financial and performance reports. This methodology includes assigning weights to factors used to score grantee and project risk. The office did not use weighting for fiscal year 2014. According to child labor

office officials, they did not use the weighting system because they determined that it did not add substantial value or affect results in a relevant manner, and that they could use a simpler approach without weighting the factors to produce results of equal value. They added that they review the risk analysis process each year and can make changes, as needed.

[26] Currently, the external auditor is the Office of the Auditor General of Canada. During the period 2005–2013, 47 ILO projects were reviewed.

[27] DOL's regulations for grants are found at 29 C.F.R. part 95.

[28] The attestation engagement report stated that conditions were deemed significant if they were systemic in nature and likely to substantially diminish program success if left unresolved, or reflected substantial noncompliance with program regulations or guidelines requiring immediate management corrective action.

[29] GAO/AIMD-00-21.3.1.

[30] Task orders are issued under existing contracts.

[31] 29 C.F.R. part 95.

[32] The grant closeout process is what takes place when the federal grantor agency determines that all applicable administrative actions and all required work of the grant have been completed by the grantee and the grantor.

[33] GAO/AIMD-00-21.3.1.

[34] The child labor office has two common indicators with project-level targets. For projects funded prior to fiscal year 2010, the common indicators were (1) the number of children withdrawn from child labor and (2) the number of children prevented from involvement with child labor. For projects funded in fiscal year 2010 or later, the common indicators are (1) the number of children engaged in or at high-risk of entering child labor who were provided educational or vocational services and (2) the number of households receiving livelihood services.

[35] According to the trade and labor office, previous common indicators include the number and percent of individuals whose economic situation has benefitted from DOL project assistance and the number and percent of workplaces exposed to DOL project assistance that have implemented new measures to prevent workplace accidents and illnesses.

[36] Government Performance and Results Act Modernization Act of 2010, Pub. L. No.111- 352, 124 Stat. 3866 (2011).

[37] We used the monitoring procedures and guidelines each office provides to grantees to identify these requirements.

[38] There was no baseline survey or targets for a project in the Maldives because, according to officials, after the project document was completed, the Maldives experienced political unrest that interfered with implementation of the project and significantly delayed project activities.

[39] According to ILAB, the child labor office and trade and labor office follow the DOL Performance Management Center's standard for meeting a target, which is that if a project has achieved 95 to 104 percent of the target for an indicator, they consider the project to have met the target.

[40] The child labor office also has a common indicator for country capacity—the number of countries with increased capacity to address child labor or forced labor. Projects provide a narrative report of project efforts and outcomes to achieve targets, for example, the adaptation of the country's legal framework to meet international labor standards. Child labor office officials said that they then assess the impact of these activities to determine whether the country counts as having increased capacity to address child labor.

[41] Of the 12 active projects with common indicators in our analysis, we excluded 3 that did not have fiscal year 2013 targets. Of the 9 active projects with fiscal year 2013 targets, we excluded 2 projects from our analysis because ILAB is working with the grantees to clarify their data.

[42] Of the 8 completed child labor projects in our sample that were active between fiscal year 2006 and fiscal year 2013, 2 projects—in Pakistan and in Lusophone Africa —did not have a midterm evaluation. Officials said that the Pakistan project's midterm evaluation was canceled because of security concerns. The Lusophone Africa project was a relatively small grant that experienced significant delays. According to officials, after the Lusophone project document was finalized, they made a decision not to conduct an internal review, given the limited duration of the project and the fact that a final evaluation was set to occur at the end of the project.

[43] For the trade and labor office, we reviewed midterm evaluations for four Better Work countries as well as an evaluation of the global Better Work program. Of the trade and labor office projects in our sample, there was no midterm evaluation for 2 projects: The Peru/Haiti project had not reached its midpoint at the time of our analysis, and there was no midterm completed for the Maldives project because it was a small project, and trade and labor office officials deemed the expense of an external evaluation would not be the best use of funds.

[44] Of the 22 child labor projects in our sample, 4 projects had attestation engagements. We also reviewed the three most recently completed attestation engagements that were not part of our sample to obtain information from the more current engagements.

[45] The 4 trade and labor office projects in our sample of 26 were still ongoing.

[46] A DOL grant officer sent a formal letter informing the grantee of the rejection, as final evaluations are part of project deliverables, with potential monetary consequences.

[47] Since 2010, the child labor office has been reporting on the number of beneficiary children who receive educational services rather than the number of children who are withdrawn and prevented from engaging in child labor. The number of children receiving educational services is an output indicator; the number of children who are withdrawn and prevented from engaging in child labor is an outcome indicator. Grantees report on the work status of beneficiary children separately to the child labor office.

[48] Child labor officials said psychosocial services are more common in projects involving children in sexually exploitative labor.

[49] Specifically, the conference report to the Consolidated Appropriations Act, 2010 directed that ILAB funds be administered in accordance with a Senate report that stated that funds may be used to support microcredit programs and other livelihood activities that contribute to a more comprehensive approach to addressing the root causes of labor exploitation, including child and forced labor (see H.R. conf. 111-366 and S. rep. 111-066).

[50] These 7 impact evaluations are for different projects than the final evaluations we reviewed and discussed previously.

[51] Child labor office officials told us they intend to elevate the issue, and the grant officer will send a formal letter to ILO regarding its commitments to DOL under the grant. During our audit work, ILAB provided us with 1 of the tracer studies, which we could not review because it is in Spanish. In August 2014, ILAB sent us 3 more tracer studies (2 in English, 1 in Spanish) published in 2012. We could not review those because they arrived after we completed our audit work.

[52] ILAB officials told us in the cases where ILAB is the only donor, there are ILAB funds being applied to the baseline studies and subsequent years of data collection.

End Notes for Appendix I

[1] GAO, *Standards for Internal Control in the Federal Government,* GAO/AIMD-00-21.3.1 (Washington, D.C.: Nov. 1,1999).

[2] We excluded 3 trade and labor office projects from the analysis because 1 project had not finalized its performance monitoring plan, 1 project did not have targets, and 1 project only had life-of-project targets.

[3] The trade and labor office projects in our sample were still ongoing at the time of our review, and thus did not yet have a final evaluation.

INDEX

D

E

F

N

O

P

Q

R

S

T

U

V

W